D1588151

ISLANDS OF
SCOTLAND

Pat Morgan

ISLANDS OF
SCOTLAND

First published in the UK in 2014

© Demand Media Limited 2014

www.demand-media.co.uk

Printed and bound in Europe

ISBN 978-1-910270-22-6

Contents

Introduction

RIGHT Lewis and Harris – one of the world's favourite islands

During the late summer and autumn of 1773, the elderly Samuel Johnson, accompanied by his friend James Boswell, journeyed throughout the islands of the Hebrides off the west coast of Scotland. The two writers travelled by horseback, coach and boat, staying with the local gentry and observing places and people that bore little resemblance to the relative comforts of the cities to which they were more accustomed. Johnson published his impressions in his 1775 volume *A Journey to the Western Islands of Scotland,* while Boswell recorded his impressions of Johnson in 1785 with the publication of *A Journal of a Tour to the Hebrides.*

The two authors were not the first travellers to be attracted to Scotland's islands by the prospect of wild beauty, splendid isola-tion and alien cultures, but they served to bring the attention of the wider world to some of the world's great wonders. They did not venture beyond the Hebrides, and thus missed out on the glories of many hundreds of islands that adorn Scotland's coast, but they provoked a desire in many a would-be tourist to visit places that, even now, can seem separated from the rest of Britain by more than just water.

The isles of Scotland, each one its own little world with its own distinct nature, form one of the world's most magical at-tractions. There are probably too many for any one traveller to explore thor-oughly in a lifetime, though some have tried. There are too many for this book to cover in detail, and the most we can hope to do is to offer some highlights of the myriad on offer.

There are, all told, more than 790 off-shore islands scattered round the 6,000 miles of Scotland's coastline. They range from the sizeable, such as Lewis and Harris in the Outer Hebrides, to tiny outcrops of rock that barely seem worthy of the name of island; from the rugged and mountainous to the lower-lying and serene; from the seemingly impossibly remote to those that are linked to the Scottish mainland by a bridge. Every single one of those islands has its own personality and character and every single one is worth a visit. If only there were the time…

Most readers will be familiar with the names of the four main groups of islands: Orkney, Shetland, the Inner Hebrides and the Outer Hebrides. Also to be taken into consideration are smaller groups of islands in the Firth of Forth, on Scotland's east coast, in the Solway Firth to the south-west and in the Firth of Clyde in the west. Many can be accessed by regular ferry or air services or bridge, while friendly boat or aircraft owners can sometimes be persuaded to drop off intrigued travellers. Most of the larger islands offer hotel accommodation and hundreds of others offer bed-and-breakfasts, campsites or hostels.

The main attractions are those that are visited by many thousands of tourists each

ABOVE
What's the story?
Tobermory, Mull

year: Skye, Mull, Arran, Lewis and Harris, Islay, some of the larger islands of Orkney and Shetland and the like. Further off the beaten tourist track are such delights as Benbecula, Colonsay, Eriskay, Great Cumbrae and Jura. Exploration of the lesser known will be rewarded handsomely.

Throughout the islands you will come across reminders of the languages that have been spoken here throughout the ages, in the names of the places you visit. Four languages have been at play in the formation of place names: English, Gaelic (still spoken, in different forms, in parts of Scotland and Ireland), Norse (a rem-

nant of the Viking era) and Brythonic (an older Celtic language than Gaelic, represented today in the Welsh and Breton tongues). Whenever you come across an island name that ends in –ay (and there are plenty of them), you will know that the Norsemen were there: it's simply the Norse word for island. English, on the other hand, took a long time to reach the islands, and its influence has been small. The Gaelic for 'island' – eilean – is widely represented, and other Gaelic words you are bound to come across include mòr (big), bàn (white) and dubh (black).

What to do once you have taken your

ferry, driven over a bridge or skimmed the waves in an aircraft to discover your island paradise? The possibilities are endless: don walking boots and new worlds will open up to you; if you're of an even more adventurous nature a spot of mountain trekking will be your thing; you might want to revel in the hospitality of the towns and villages that dot the islands, taking in a bit of local culture; perhaps you will want to marvel at your island's rewarding wildlife, explore a historic castle or two or even bask in a gorgeous sunset on a white-sanded beach.

Maybe you will want to discover a mys-

terious prehistoric site. You will doubtless be keen to sample the local cuisine and take a dram or several of some of the finest whiskies Scotland has to offer, each possessing a character all of its own. Perhaps you will be content to sit and wonder at the landscape that presents itself – mountain or moorland, loch or river, cliff or beach – or marvel at the majesty of the sea.

Confirmation that the Scottish isles offer a world of possibilities came in 2014 when travellers voted three of them – Lewis and Harris, Mainland Orkney and the Isle of Mull – into the top 10 in awards for islands in Europe, and Lewis and Harris into fifth place in the global pantheon. Those voters, wise people all, preferred the cliffs and beaches of Lewis and Harris to the wonders of the Seychelles; the Neolithic remains and gorgeous scenery of Orkney to the charms of the Balearic Islands; the multicoloured main street of Tobermory, Mull's principal town, to anything the Canaries have to offer.

In sun and rain, in summer or winter, night or day, the islands of Scotland have something for everyone who has romance in their soul, as the following pages will show. We will start our journey around the coast of Scotland in the far south-west but first examine their history and geography.

Chapter 1

History &
Geography

The story of the islands that form a rocky ring around Scotland mirrors in many ways the story of Scotland itself.

Some scholars believe that early humans inhabited parts of the country as early as 40,000 years ago, although the evidence for that theory is scant. Following the retreat of the mighty glaciers that covered much of Britain during the last Ice Age, around 15,000 years ago, humans began to inhabit Scotland in meaningful numbers, and flint artefacts around 12,000 years old have been found in what is now Lanarkshire. The first signs of settled habitation, dated to 8,500 years ago, have been discovered near Edinburgh on the mainland. Although there is evidence of domesticity, these early Scots seem to have been mobile and may have moved from site to site as the seasons changed. They used boats for transport and fishing and moved inland from the coasts to hunt using stone weapons.

As time went on through the Neolithic age, these people began to settle down into farming communities, clearing forests for crops and keeping domestic animals. Pottery and other artefacts of these people have been found throughout the islands, and buildings remain too. A stone-built, chambered tomb discovered at Maeshowe on Orkney features a carefully aligned entrance passageway that allowed sunshine to illuminate the main chamber at the winter solstice. A well-preserved stone settlement at Skara Brae on Orkney, dating from 3200BC, shows that covered passageways connected the houses.

With the coming of the Iron Age, in ap-

proximately 700BC, the people inhabiting Scotland and its islands started to trade and use new technologies. These were Celtic people who took the decoration of metalwork to extraordinarily beautiful lengths, wore colourful clothes and jew-ellery and produced remarkably intricate knot patterns on stone and other materi-als. Soon the Roman Empire began to stretch towards Britain, and the Romans came to call the Celtic tribes in the north Caledoni, and their land Caledonia.

ABOVE Neolithic chambered tomb at Maeshowe, Orkney

ABOVE Prehistoric settlement at Skara Brae, Orkney

The Romans named one of the tribes, who painted or tattooed their bodies, the Picts (the 'painted people'). The Picts are perpetuated in the names of towns deriving from their language, such as Urquhart (by the thicket) and Aberdeen (mouth of the Don).

After the Roman conquest of Britain, the tribes of Caledonia fought hard to keep the invaders out of their territory;

for their part, the Romans were keen to keep the tribes out of the south. In efforts to keep the peace they built two mighty fortifications: Hadrian's Wall, which was begun in 122AD and extended from Wallsend in the east to the Solway Firth in the west; and the Antonine Wall, which stretched between the Firth of Forth and the Firth of Clyde. The latter, completed around 155AD, marked the northern extremity of the Roman Empire.

The Romans had finally abandoned Britain by around 410AD, by which time Christianity had been brought to the islands by Saint Ninian, who founded a mission at Whithorn in Galloway around 397AD. From here missionaries set forth to convert the Picts in the furthest flung islands, reaching as far as St Ninian's Isle in Shetland. The work was carried on in notable fashion by the Irish abbot and missionary Saint Columba, who landed on Iona in the Inner Hebrides in 563AD and went on to found the Celtic Church. But the monks carrying out this missionary work were eventually driven from Iona by peoples who had a profound influence on the history of Scotland: the Vikings.

The men in the longships began their raids on Scottish territory in the eighth century, and religious establishments were often prime targets. By 807 Iona had suffered a bloody attack in which 68 monks were slaughtered and their lovingly assembled library was looted. By the late ninth century Orkney had been colonised by Norsemen and parts of the Hebrides were home to peoples of mixed Norse and Gaelic blood.

It was in the 11th century that the Viking kingdom of the Isle of Man and the Sudreys (Southern Isles) was established, and by 1153 the Norse-Gaelic warlord Somerled had claimed the Lordship of the Isles from the Scottish crown. In support of the struggle for independence, castles were built in strategic west-coast locations, and the powerful Lords of the Isles remained effectively independent of Scotland for several centuries. It wasn't until the end of the 15th century that the Lordship came to an end, when John Macdonald II forfeited his estates to James IV of Scotland.

Meanwhile, the history of Scotland as a whole had been characterised for centuries by blood-spattered disputes over sovereignty. In 1295 King John entered into an alliance with France, known ever after as the Auld Alliance. English invasion, under the leadership of Edward I, followed. Scottish landowner Sir William

HISTORY & GEOGRAPHY

RIGHT St Ninian's
Isle, Shetland

Wallace came to the fore as a military leader and defeated an English army at the Battle of Stirling Bridge in 1297.

Wallace served as Guardian of Scotland until his defeat at the Battle of Falkirk the following year. He initially escaped the clutches of the English but was captured near Glasgow in 1305 and handed over to Edward. The rest will be familiar to those who have watched the otherwise historically dubious film *Braveheart*. Wallace was hanged, drawn and quartered for high treason, despite the fact that he owed no allegiance to England.

Robert Bruce was appointed joint Guardian with John Comyn in Wallace's place, and was promoted to King in 1306, soon after having participated in Comyn's murder. Bruce inflicted a significant defeat on the English under Edward II at the Battle of Bannockburn in 1314, securing a kind of independence in the process.

Soon after, an intervention by the Pope allowed Scotland's sovereignty to be recognised by the major dynasties of Europe. The year 1326 saw what was perhaps the first full session of the Parliament of Scotland, and two years later Edward III signed the treaty of Northampton, acknowledging independence under the rule of Robert the Bruce.

But it was only four years before the English invaded again, giving rise to the Second War of Independence. Their efforts to install Edward Balliol on the Scottish throne failed, and in 1371 the first of the Stuart (or Stewart) kings, Robert II, came to power. Nine Stuart monarchs were to rule Scotland before 1603, when further powers were to come the dynasty's way.

During the reigns of those kings, much of great importance occurred in Scotland and its islands that served to help form the country we know today. In 1468, for example, James III married Margaret of Denmark, receiving the Orkney Islands and the Shetland Islands by way of a dowry. While Berwick-upon-Tweed was lost to the English in 1482, further territory came the way of Scotland six years later when James IV ended the semi-independent rule of the Lord of the Isles to bring the Western Isles under the monarch's rule for the first time. An indicator of future events came in 1503, when the same James married Margaret Tudor, the daughter of Henry VII of England.

The reign of James IV witnessed a great flowering of Scottish culture as the influence of the European Renaissance grew. The 15th century also saw significant

ABOVE Prehistoric and Norse settlement, Shetland

developments in the field of education with the founding of three universities and the passing of the Education Act, with its decree that the sons of barons and important freeholders should attend grammar schools.

In 1512 the Auld Alliance between Scotland and France was renewed and the following year, when England under Henry VIII attacked the French, James IV retaliated with an invasion of England. The result was the disastrous Battle of Flodden Field, at which the king and around ten thousand Scottish troops were killed – a bloody event that is commemorated in the song *Flowers of the Forest*.

Further Stuart sorties against England culminated in the Battle of Solway Moss in 1542 – another defeat for Scotland and, apparently, so hard for James V to take that he died of a broken heart. The day before his death he was told of the birth of a daughter, the girl who would grow up to become Mary, Queen of Scots.

Mary was brought up in Catholic France and married the Dauphin, who became Francis II of that country. When her husband died Mary returned to Scotland to wear the crown. Her reign was notable for the number of crises it endured. They were largely provoked by the Catholic nobles of Scotland, who disapproved of Mary's reluctance to impose her and their religion on the populace.

Married successively to Lord Darnley (who was murdered) and the Earl of Bothwell (who was implicated in the murder), she was eventually taken and imprisoned by Bothwell's rivals. Languishing in Loch Leven Castle, Mary was forced to abdicate in 1567, and the crown passed to her infant son, who became James VI. While the intrigues continued, Mary escaped and fled to England, where she became the focal point for Catholic conspirators. Tried for treason on the orders of Elizabeth I, Mary was executed in 1587.

Meanwhile, Scotland had been undergoing a religious revolution under the influence of Calvinism. The country's Parliament had adopted in 1560 a confession of faith that rejected the Mass and the jurisdiction of the Pope. In England, Henry VIII had separated the Church of England from Rome in 1534.

In 1603, following the death of Elizabeth I without an heir, James VI of Scotland acceded to the English throne, thus also becoming James I of England. The crowns of the two countries remained separate, despite James's efforts to create a throne of Great Britain. The acquisition of Irish sovereignty allowed Protestant Scots to settle in the province of Ulster.

There followed a period of great unrest and bloodshed throughout Scotland. It was not until 1660, after the English Civil War, the Commonwealth of Oliver Cromwell and the restoration of Charles II to the throne that Scotland became once again an independent kingdom. Under James VII (James II of England), the last Catholic to reign in Britain, Protestant subjects were alienated, and William of Orange was invited by leading Englishmen to land with an army and claim the throne. James fled, in what became known as the Glorious Revolution.

James's supporters (Jacobites) could not accept the status quo and there followed a series of risings against the crown. The revolution was decisively put down at the Battle of Dunkeld in 1689, but there was more to come. Thirty-eight members of the Clan MacDonald were massacred in Glen Coe, in the Highlands, by the Earl of Argyll's Regiment of Foot because they had not pledged allegiance to William and his wife Mary (the daughter of James VII) quickly enough.

Finally, the kingdoms of Scotland and England were united politically and economically by the Acts of Union of 1707. With Wales, the countries now formed the new nation of Great Britain.

The Jacobite cause, however, continued to play a major role in the affairs of the new state. Jacobites found the union unacceptable, and their efforts to wrest control of the throne from the Hanoverian dynasty culminated in the military campaigns of Charles Edward Stuart, better known as Bonnie Prince Charlie

or the Young Pretender. With the support of several clans he took Edinburgh and Carlisle and marched as far south as Derby before retreating to Scotland. Pursued further and further north by the Duke of Cumberland – known as the Butcher – Charles and his army were finally routed at the Battle of Culloden, east of Inverness, in 1746. The Jacobites had been crushed, with Charles managing to flee to Skye in the Hebrides with the aid of Flora MacDonald, and thence escape to France

The 18th century in Scotland saw the beginning of a great outpouring of Scottish intellectual and scientific genius. The Enlightenment then in full flower in Europe flourished likewise in Scotland, and there were huge advances in the arts, philosophy, economics, medicine, architecture, law, agriculture and many other fields of human accomplishment. By 1750, Scotland could boast a literacy level of around 75 per cent, making its citizens some of Europe's most literate people, and this was the time when names such as Robert Burns (writer), Adam Smith (economist), Joseph Black (physicist and chemist) and James Hutton (the first modern geologist) came to the fore. There were many others.

The Union with England and Wales also brought Scotland massive economic and commercial benefits, and the coming Industrial Revolution helped to transform the country from the poor agricultural society it had been in 1750 into one of Europe's leading industrial powerhouses. The country's population grew rapidly in the 19th century and alongside the explosion in population came a blooming of Scotland's industrial powers as it became a world force in shipbuilding, engineering and locomotive and railway construction, helped by its many entrepreneurs and engineers and ready supplies of easily mined coal.

Worldwide economic depression followed the war, and it hit Scotland particularly hard. Unemployment was high, political agitation widespread, and the government was fearful of an uprising, at one point deploying tanks and troops in the centre of Glasgow. Resistance had turned to passive despair by the end of the 1920s but, with all the main political parties committed to the Union, new groupings began to emerge. The Scottish National Party (SNP) was formed in 1934 with the express aim of recreating an independent Scotland.

Following World War II, the country's economic and social fortunes took another nosedive as overseas competition and industrial unrest took their toll. But a corner was turned in the 1970s with the exploitation of gas and oil in the North Sea – with islands to the north of Scotland among the beneficiaries – and the turning of the economy away from heavy industry and towards the service sector. There were renewed calls for Scottish independence, or at least devolution of powers from London to Edinburgh, but a referendum on devolution in 1979 proved unsuccessful for the nationalists. Nevertheless, the SNP was by now a significant force in British politics.

When the Labour Party was returned to power in 1997, the way became clear for change. A further referendum confirmed that the Scottish people wanted devolved powers, and the Scottish Parliament duly opened for business in 1999.

As we have already seen, Scotland can boast 790 offshore islands, of which 89 were recorded as having a resident population in 2011. They are mainly to be found in four main groups – the Inner and Outer Hebrides, Shetland and Orkney – and further clusters in the Solway

Firth and the Firth of Clyde, off the west coast, and the Firth of Forth in the east.

The landscapes of the islands are widely varied, the result of important influential geological factors at play in different eras of the Earth's history. Archaean Lewisian gneiss, formed three billion years ago, forms the bedrock of a good number of the islands, while 400 million-year-old Old Red Sandstone is the basis of Shapinsay and other islands in Orkney. Rum and others like it were formed from volcanic activity in the Tertiary geological period, between 66 and 2.5 million years ago. This variety of influences has produced landscapes such as the glorious mountain ranges of Skye and the low-lying terrains of its neighbour Tiree and islands in Orkney.

The islands are no less varied in terms of size. Lewis and Harris is the largest, measuring up at just over 2,000 square kilometres, while at the other end of the scale are tiny outcrops of rock like Staffa in the Inner Hebrides, with an area of just 33 hectares.

The human geography of the islands has changed much over the centuries. Today, Lewis and Harris is home to a population of 21,000, a figure that has stayed fairly constant for 150 years, and the number of inhabitants of the islands as a whole is more than 100,000. But it is a sad fact that many smaller islands that once had thriving populations are uninhabited today. The notorious Highland Clearances of the 18th and 19th centuries, when tenants were forced from their homes by owners intent on enclosing their lands for their own use, resulted in many an island losing its residents. Another major factor in the loss of population came in the form of emigration to the new world in the 18th and 19th centuries.

There are signs of a regrowth in population, however. In the 10 years leading up to the Census of 2011, the number of inhabitants of the islands grew by four per cent whereas it had fallen by three per cent between 1991 and 2001. The increase was particularly noticeable in the Western Isles, where local people now own around two thirds of the land. Where community ownership is less evident, populations continue to fall.

The names of Scotland's islands provide indicators of their histories. In the Northern Isles, where the presence of the Norse people was most strongly felt, place names reflect the influence of the Vikings and their successors, while further south in the Western Isles, Scots Gaelic names are more common. The Northmen left their mark on the culture of the islands, too; perhaps the most notable can be seen in the form of Up Helly Aa, annual fire festivals that take place in Shetland and involve the burning of a Viking galley. Fascinating traces of ancient languages abound throughout the islands.

Most of the islands are subject to unsubtle attentions from the weather systems of the oceans in which they lie. Rain is sometimes perceived as a constant companion off the west coast of Scotland, and many islands are bleak, inhospitable places during wild winters, although it should be noted that many a glorious summer day can be spent idling on a beautiful beach. There are also many strong tides, and sailors learn to steer clear of notorious whirlpools such as Corryvreckan, a tidal race between Jura and Scarba that is said to be the world's third largest.

This brief survey of the history and make-up of the islands of Scotland provides a mere taster for a tour of some of the country's most prized assets. More rewards lie in store as we delve into each group of islands in turn.

Chapter 2

The Solway Firth & the Firth of Clyde

The Solway Firth, where English waters meet Scottish, doesn't at first sight appear to have much to offer the island spotter, but what it does have turns out to be fascinating.

The tiny Hestan Island measures just 460 by 270 metres and is sometimes accessible, depending on the tides, by foot from Almorness Point. At its southern end is a series of pinnacles that rejoice in the name of Daft Anne's Steps; it's said that a local lass drowned here while laying stepping stones in an attempt to reach Alcary Point. Hestan's south-western coast features caves that served as storage spaces for smugglers of the 18th century.

North of Hestan lies another island that can sometimes be reached by foot from the mainland – check the tide ta-bles carefully. Rough Island has been a bird sanctuary since 1937, and visitors should avoid the island during the nesting months of May and June.

Travel northwards around the west coast of Scotland and you will come to the Firth of Clyde, just a few miles from the conurbation that surrounds Glasgow. These waters are home to the 40 islands and skerries (small rocky islands) that make up the country's fifth largest group; just four of them are inhabited by humans.

The largest of these islands is Arran, which has a population of nearly 5,000 and an area of 43,000 hectares. Viewed from the Ayrshire coast, the north of the island presents a range of hills known as the Sleeping Warrior because of their resemblance to a recumbent man. Arran's highest point, Goatfell, measures up at

ABOVE Summit of the 874m Goatfell, Arran

874 metres and is a popular attraction for visitors.

Arran is often called Scotland in Miniature, for it is divided into 'Highland' and 'Lowland' areas by the Highland Boundary Fault that runs across the country. This island is a piece of paradise for geologists, who travel from afar to inspect igneous landforms like sills and dykes, and rocks dating from the Precambrian era during which the Earth was formed, about 4,600 million years ago.

Arran has several villages, the most obvious of which is Brodick, where the ferry from the mainland docks and where Brodick Castle – seat of the Dukes of Hamilton – can be found. The largest village on the island is Lamlash, home to the island's schools, hospital and local government offices.

Another Firth of Clyde island that is divided into 'Highland' and 'Lowland' is Bute, considerably smaller in size than Arran at 12,000 hectares but with a larger population of 6,500. This is one of Scotland's most accessible islands, being just a short ferry ride from Wemyss Bay on the mainland. The only town on Bute, Rothesay, is the location of the 13th century Rothesay Castle, notable for its circular plan – the only one in Scotland. Restored by the Marquess of Bute in the 1800s, the castle was given to the state and is in the care of Historic Scotland.

If you're a fan of beautiful beaches, you will want to head for the western side of Bute. Here you can luxuriate in splendid views over the Sound of Bute towards Arran and the small island of Inchmarnock. The northern part of Bute is rugged and sparsely populated but has an alternative ferry port at Rhubodach that is a mere 300 metres from the mainland.

The third most populous island in the Firth of Clyde is Great Cumbrae, whose Gaelic name, Cumaradh Mòr, simply means large island of the Cymric people, recalling the previous Brythonic-speaking folk of the ancient Kingdom of Strathclyde. The island has an area of 1,168 hectares and a population, in 2011, of 1,376.

Great Cumbrae, like Ireland, has its legendary scourge of snakes. In this case it was not Saint Patrick who drove the serpents off an island but St Mirin, who is said to have accomplished the feat in the eighth century. On the site where the saint is said to have preached, in the island's main town of Millport, can be found the Cathedral of the Isles, a beautiful but tiny church completed in 1851. Also on a small scale is The Wedge, a private house with the UK's smallest frontage – the width of a front door.

Great Cumbrae's smaller neighbour is, reasonably enough, Little Cumbrae, an isle of 313 hectares. Unlike its fertile big brother, Little Cumbrae is a rocky place whose cliffs are more in keeping with those of a Hebridean island further north than the other Firth of Clyde islands.

Further out to sea – indeed 10 miles from the mainland – can be found the dramatic outline of Ailsa Craig, formed from the volcanic plug of an extinct volcano. The source of blue hone granite used to make curling stones, this mysterious, unforgettable island rises to nearly 350m and merits its name, which comes from the Gaelic for 'fairy rock'.

Ailsa Craig also rejoices in the nickname of Paddy's Milestone, being roughly halfway between Belfast and Glasgow on the route taken by Irish labourers seeking work in Scotland in times past. Once a place of refuge for Catholics during the Scottish Reformation, the island is now a bird sanctuary inhabited by thousands of gannets, some of which find its slopes a little vertiginous.

Also important for its birdlife is Sanda, a

ABOVE The Fairy Rock – Ailsa Craig

127-hectare island off the southern tip of the Kintyre Peninsula. Privately owned, Sanda is known to the people of Arran as Spoon Island because of its resemblance to an up-turned utensil. Another point of interest lies in the legend that Saint Ninian, the first evangeliser north of Hadrian's Wall, was buried here and that anyone who stepped on his grave, marked by an alder tree, would die. Sanda's former owners include Jack Bruce, bass player in the legendary rock group Cream, and the retailer James Gulliver, founder of the Argyll Group.

Leaving the sheltered waters of the Firth of Clyde, we round the southern-most tip of the Mull of Kintyre and turn north towards the more exposed yet mild climate of the Inner Hebrides.

Chapter 3

The Inner Hebrides

The islands, nearly 80 of them, that make up the Inner Hebrides provide Scotland with one of its most precious assets and pull countless thousands of visitors from all over the globe. This is an archipelago of wild, untamed beauty, mountainous in parts, low-lying in others. Its mild, friendly climate, stunning vistas and air of mystery have attracted artists, musicians and writers for centuries and its characterful whiskies have fanatical followers throughout the world.

First, the facts. The Inner Hebrides chain is composed of 35 inhabited islands – the best-known of them being perhaps Skye, Mull, Islay, Rum, Eigg and Tiree – and a further 44 that are uninhabited but have an area of over 30 hectares. The 2011 Census found the Inner Hebridean population standing at nearly 19,000, a few hundred more than 10 years previously. Of those, more than half live on the Isle of Skye.

The Scottish Gaelic language and culture are strong influences on the character of these islands: in 1921 more than half of the populations of most were Gaelic speakers, although by 2001 only a third of Skye residents and 48 per cent of Tiree people could speak the language.

Next, an examination in detail of some of these enchanted isles. Naturally, it's not possible to cover every Inner Hebridean island in these pages; what follows can only give a flavour of some of the larger and better known.

At the southern end of the Inner Hebrides, lying a mere 40 kilometres from the northern coast of Ireland, is Islay, often called the Queen of the Hebrides and at one time 'capital' of the Western Isles. Islay (pronounced Isla) is in fact the fifth largest of Scotland's islands at 62,000 hectares, and has a thriving population of more than 3,000. You may travel here from the mainland by ferry or air.

This is an island of contrasts, with a mountainous east coast facing the Mull of Kintyre away to the east and Jura to the north, with lower-lying, fertile areas to the

ABOVE Water of life – Bruichladdich distillery, Islay

ABOVE Loch a' Bhaile Mhargaidh, Jura

south and west. Islay is also an island with an unparalleled reputation for producing the water of life, or uisge beatha as Scottish Gaelic has it. Whisky has been produced on Islay – or produced legally, at any rate – since 1779, and at one time the island could boast no fewer than 23 distilleries.

Nowadays there are just the eight distilleries to choose from, and the quality of the whiskies they produce is unrivalled. Distilleries on the south of the island produce powerful, peaty whiskies such as Lagavulin, Laphroaig and Ardbeg, while

those in the north – Bowmore, Bruichladdich, Bunnahabhain and Caol Ila – are known for their lighter malts. There is even a recently opened microdistillery, Kilchoman, on the west coast.

It's near this distillery, in the Rinns peatbog, now a nature reserve, that huge flocks of barnacle, greylag and Greenland white-fronted geese gather every winter, providing quite a spectacle for wildlife-hungry visitors. Rinns is separated from the rest of Islay by an isthmus between Loch Indaal and Loch Gruinart, and it

was at the head of the latter that a savage battle was fought in 1598 by the Mac-Leans of Duart and the MacDonalds of Islay. MacDonalds claim to this day that their victory came thanks to the aid of the Du-sith, the black elf.

The north and east of the island are ideal for a spot of hill walking, and it's also here that Loch Finlaggan, one of Scotland's most important archaeological sites, can be found. Two crannogs (artificial islands) in the loch are covered with ruins, reminders of the time when the loch was the Lord of the Isles' headquarters. Nearly 30 buildings have been excavated, among them the Great Hall of the Lords, a chapel and buildings that held the 'parliament' of religious and temporal leaders.

Turning south past Bridgend, site of the former laird's house, one comes to the village of Port Charlotte, built at the turn of the 18th century and known as the Queen of the Rinns. Here every house is identical to its neighbour and measures nine by seven metres. Further on

are Bowmore, the island's 'capital', and Port Ellen, the main centre of population. Turn south or east from here and you will find more whisky country and then, in the east, Kildalton High Cross, thought by many to be the finest example of a Celtic cross in the whole of Scotland. Standing by a ruined chapel, it was carved out of bluestone in around 800AD.

You want wild landscapes, perfect peace and isolation, rocky peaks and rough, boggy lowland? You want a taste of some of the finest whisky money can buy? Then you'll want to travel to Jura, which sometimes appears to be untouched by human hand.

Jura is an island of 37,000 hectares and around 200 hardy souls separated from Islay's east coast by a narrow sound. Most visitors arrive by ferry from Islay, although it's also possible to travel from the mainland. This is the Inner Hebrides' most untamed island, much of it devoid of signs of human habitation but home to red deer, golden eagles and busy otters. It proved inspirational for the author George Orwell, who found refuge here while writing *Nineteen Eighty-Four* towards the end of his life. And it's dominated by two of nature's most aptly named mountains: the Paps of Jura.

They may be breast-shaped but, oddly enough, there are three Paps: Beinn an Òir (mountain of gold, 785 metres), Beinn Shiantaidh (holy mountain, 755 metres) and Beinn a' Chaolais (mountain of the kyle, or strait, 734 metres). If you're the energetic type you'll be glad to know the Paps can be scaled (after taking the usual precautions; the weather can be changeable), the effort you expend being recompensed by a drop of malt afterwards; you may also be staggered to learn that people actually *run* up and down these peaks during the annual Jura Fell Race.

The aforementioned gorgeous whisky, named after the island, is distilled in the only settlement worthy of the name, Craighouse, which sits on Jura's southeast coast. Here you will also find a hotel, a post office and shop, and not much more. What more could you need in such surroundings? Carry on southwards and you will find Jura House, which has superb gardens that are open to the public.

The twin islands of Colonsay and Oronsay lie west of Jura and are themselves separated by a narrow expanse of shell sand, called The Strand, over which you can walk when the tide is out. Legend has it that a fugitive from Colonsay was safe from punishment once he reached a

LEFT Beach on Colonsay

sanctuary cross halfway across, provided he stayed on Oronsay for a year and a day.

Colonsay is an island of some 4,000 hectares and has a population around the 150 mark; inhabitants of the much smaller Oronsay were counted at just eight in 2011. But people have been living here for a very long time: Neolithic flint tools and animal bones excavated at Kiloran Bay on the north-west coast of Colonsay have been dated to 8,700 years ago. Other finds have included the remains of a Viking ship burial of 855AD in which the warrior was interred with his weapons, horse and coins.

Colonsay's main settlement is Scalasaig on the east coast, from where ferries sail to Oban on the mainland. Not to be outdone by its whisky-distilling neighbours, Colonsay produces beer in Scalasaig, making it the smallest island in the world with its own brewery. The Colonsay Brewery proudly claims to employ 10 per cent of the island's workforce – Chris and Bob.

Across The Strand on Oronsay can be seen the ruins of an Augustinian priory said to be second in importance to Iona. Saint Columba, the sixth century Irish abbot and missionary who is credited with spreading Christianity in Scotland, is believed to have rejected this island in favour of the latter because it was within sight of his native Ireland, but the priory – a whole group of buildings in a decent state of preservation – is an interesting place to visit. Built around 1380, perhaps on the site of a monastery of Saint Oran of 563AD, the priory features two memorable Celtic crosses.

Oronsay is normally a placid place, but the peace is disturbed when roaring grey seal bulls proclaim their dominance from the outlying skerries in the autumn.

North of Jura, clinging to the mainland, lie the Slate Islands, so named because of the Dalradian slate that forms their basis and was quarried from the 17th until the middle of the 20th century. Indeed, there was once more to this group of islands than exists today: Easdale or Eilean-a-beithich (island of the birches) was quarried to a depth of 76 metres below sea level, and the remaining outer rim was largely destroyed by the waves.

Seil (population: 550), the most northerly of the islands, has been linked to the mainland by the Clachan Bridge since 1793. Here you will find the former slate-

mining village of Ellenabeich, also known as Easdale, which takes its name from the neighbouring island and features a heritage centre operated by the Scottish Slate Islands Trust. The picturesque village was used as a location for the filming of *Ring of Bright Water*.

South of Seil lies Luing (population: 200), which provided the slate for the roof of Iona Cathedral but is now better known as the home of a breed of beef cattle and of one of Scotland's largest lobster fishing centre.

Near the village of Toberonochy can be found the ruin of Kilchatton chapel, surrounded by slate gravestones. One stone announces that the grave's resident 'digged my grave before I died' and goes on to warn against a multitude of people, including 'women that wear Babylonish garments' and 'men that have whiskers'. In the middle of Luing is the Fairy Knoll, on which visitors are required to place a hair in order to appease the wee folk.

The uninhabited Lunga, to the west of Luing, is nowadays the scene of adventure courses for youngsters. To its south, between Lunga and Scarba, is the 200-metre wide Bealach a' Choin Ghlais, through which streams the notorious Grey Dog tidal race. It was described in 1845 as '…

ISLANDS OF SCOTLAND

ABOVE Rubha nan Gall lighthouse, Mull, with ferry and Ardnamurchan peninsula in the background

about one cable broad, and the stream of water during the greater part of ebb and flood rushes along the narrow pass with much violence. So great is the overfall on the current that even during moderate tides it is impossible to force a boat through.' The Grey Dog is sometimes called 'Little Corryvreckan' because of its resemblance to the infamous tidal race between Scarba and Jura.

Scarba itself, set between two such violent tidal systems, consists largely of a single mountain that rises to 449 metres. It is no longer permanently inhabited but once had such a reputation for healthy living that when the death of an old lady was recorded in the 17th century her age was given as 140.

❖━━•━━•━━━━◆━━━━•━━•━━❖

The Firth of Lorn lies between Mull and the mainland and contains islands well worth a visit. Lismore is worthy of its name, which means big garden, for its long, narrow shape offers undulating walks in shallow valleys and its fertile soil encourages a profusion of trees, shrubs and wild flowers.

Lismore has an area of 2,351 hectares and was home to a population of 192 in 2011. Its highest point is Barr Mòr at 127 metres, which affords heavenly panoramic views from its summit.

Legends abound here, and it should not be a surprise to learn that some of it concerns Saint Columba. Apparently he was in a race with his contemporary Saint Moluag to become the first to found a monastery on Lismore. The first saint to touch the island would be the winner. Moluag, realising he was about to lose, cut off his finger and hurled it ashore, earning him the right to establish his monastery in 564AD. Competitive, these saints.

Kerrera (1,200 hectares; population 57), another island of the Firth of Lorn, lies close to Oban, for whose harbour it provides a breakwater. A quiet place with lovely walks, it is known for its ruined Gylen Castle, which sits alone on a promontory overlooking the firth. The castle, built in 1587 by Duncan MacDougall of Dunollie, was besieged and burned in 1647 by the Covenanter General David Leslie. It was here that the MacDougalls' Brooch of Lorn – an 11cm disc of silver with a central dome hiding a cavity for sacred relics, said to have belonged to Robert the Bruce – was kept before being removed for safekeeping to Oban.

Seemingly falling off the end of the Morvern peninsula are the Isle of Mull and the group of islands associated with it, which include Coll, Tiree, Iona and Ulva. Mull itself is the second largest of the Inner Hebrides after Skye with an area of 875 square kilometres and a population of 2,800, swollen in summer by hordes of visitors.

In keeping with the nature of the Scottish isles, Mull has a deeply indented coastline, which, if you took the trouble to measure it, would be found to be 480 kilometres. At its core, Mull is mountainous, its highest point being the 966 metre Ben More, the highest peak in the Hebrides outside Skye. From the centre a series of peninsulas, mostly composed of moorland, spread out and on one of these, the Aros peninsula in the north-east, is found the principal town of Tobermory.

With its multi-coloured harbour front,

Tobermory (from the Gaelic for Mary's well) must by now be the best known of Hebridean towns. Used as the location for the children's TV series *Balamory*, it has also found fame as the name of a Womble in the books by Elisabeth Beresford, as the location of the 1945 Powell and Pressburger film *I Know Where I'm Going*, as the name of a cat in short stories by Saki and as the inspiration for the fictional town of Torbay in the Alistair McLean novel *When Eight Bells Toll*. Tobermory Bay is reputedly the site of the wreck of a galleon from the Spanish Armada, destroyed following the casting of a spell by a local witch and containing, according to different versions of the tale, either a fortune in gold bullion or merely the remains of her crew.

Mull's only whisky takes its name from Tobermory, where the distillery has been active, apart from a few periods of closure, since 1798. The 10-year-old single malt provides a gentle mouthful and is used for blended whiskies.

Ferries from Oban arrive at Craignure, having passed the stately and prominent Duart Castle, home of MacLeans since about 1250. Opposite the castle sits Lady's Rock, where the 11th MacLean chieftain, Lachlan Cattanach, had his wife tied up at the mercy of the tide after concluding that their marriage had failed. Lachlan was later surprised to find the mistreated woman at her brother's house, to where she had been taken after being rescued by a fisherman. The matter was not mentioned and Lachlan lived until 1527, when he was found murdered in his bed in Edinburgh.

Another castle, that of Torosay, is to be found a short distance south of Craignure. It's possible to walk through its beautiful gardens including formal terraces and a statue walk containing 19 statues that were shipped from Italy. Another point of interest on Mull is the mausoleum of Lachlan Macquarie, the governor of New South Wales from 1809 until 1822 and known as the 'Father of Australia'. It's to be found in the village of Gruline, in the central 'neck' of Mull. Macquarie was a native of the neighbouring island of Ulva.

There simply isn't enough space here to describe all of Mull's many attractions, but one of them, if you're in the mood for a walk, can be found near Carsaig, on the western peninsula known as the Ross of Mull. The Nun's Cave, where nuns from Iona are said to have hidden during the Reformation, has interesting early Christian carvings. Another long walk will bring you to Malcolm's Point, where you will

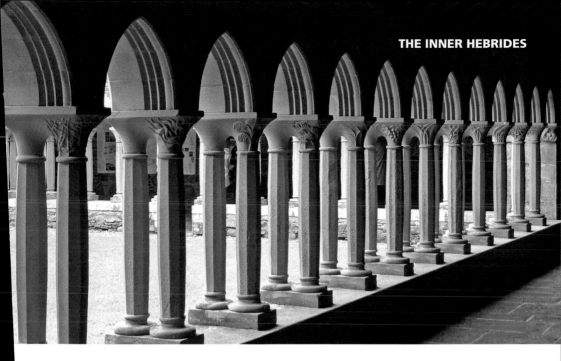

find the amazing rock formations of Carsaig Arches, eroded sea caves adjoining 220 metre high cliffs lined with basalt columns.

The small island of Iona lies off the western tip of the Ross of Mull. This 877 hectare island's Gaelic name is Ì Chaluim Chille and refers to the monastery of Saint Columba, or Colm Cille. He is thought to have founded a monastery here in 563AD after having been exiled from Ireland. Iona became a famed centre of learning, and it's possible that the Book of Kells, nowadays to be seen in Dublin's Trinity College, was started in its scriptorium towards the end of the eighth century. Nowadays, Iona Abbey is an ecumenical church and a centre of attraction for both pilgrims and tourists, who can skip over to the island on a short ferry ride from Mull.

Iona's population in 2011 was 177, most of them living in the main settlement, Baile Mòr, at St Roan's Bay on the east of the island. On the other side is Camas Cuil an t-Saimh (Bay at the Back of the Ocean), so

ABOVE Iona Abbey, one of Europe's oldest religious centres

ABOVE Fingal's
Cave, Staffa

named because the next stop on a journey westward is North America.

Separated from Mull's north-west coast by a narrow strait and connected to the small island of Gometra by a bridge is Ulva, which boasts columns on basalt rock in places – of which more anon.

James Boswell, writing in the 18th century, felt there was nothing worthy of observation on Ulva (whose name comes from the Old Norse for wolf island), but he was very wrong. Sir Walter Scott was inspired by the island to write his poem *The Lord of the Isles* in 1815, and it also has connections with the explorer David Livingstone. As we've seen, the 'father of Australia', Lachlan MacQuarie, was born here in 1761. Ulva, which measures up at nearly 2,000 hectares, has in fact been inhabited by man since Neolithic times, and at one time its population stood at 800. Sadly, it had fallen to 11 by 2011.

Rather less habitable is Staffa, which lies about 10 kilometres west of Mull and was once part of the Ulva Estate but has been uninhabited since about 1800. Its magnificent hexagonal basalt columns reminded Vikings of their houses, which were built from vertical tree logs, and bestowed the name meaning 'stave island'.

This spectacular, 33 hectare, 42 metre high island, and its main sea cave in particular, inspired Felix Mendelssohn to compose his Hebrides Overture in 1830. Its most remarkable feature became known as Fingal's Cave following the publication of an epic poem, recounting the story of Irish hero Fionn MacCool, by James Macpherson in the 18th century. Fingal, the Scots' version of the hero's name, means chief of valour. Fingal's Cave may be viewed from the sea on a sightseeing cruise or by landing elsewhere on the island and walking overland.

Way out to the west of Mull sit the islands of Coll (7,700 hectares; population 200) and Tiree (7,800 hectares; population 653). Known for its reputation as one of Britain's sunniest spots, for its sandy beaches and dunes and for its corncrakes, Coll was home to a branch of the MacLeans for half a millennium. Hostilities with other branches were never far from the surface, and they reached a peak in 1593 with a battle at Breachacha Castle against the MacLeans of Duart, who fancied the island for themselves. The Coll MacLeans managed to repel their invader cousins, and marked their triumph by decapitating the vanquished warriors and throwing the heads in a stream. The burn has been known ever since as Struthan nan Ceann – Stream of the Heads.

Coll is the home of more fascinating lore. At Ben Hogh, the island's highest peak at 106 metres, sits an enormous boulder balanced on three smaller rocks, supposedly placed there by a giant.

Tiree lies to the south-west of Coll – it is in fact the most westerly of the Inner Hebrides. Enjoying as much sunshine as its neighbour, it can also be a fairly windy place, and is consequently a popular destination for windsurfers. This is a fertile island that deserves its reputation as a land of corn, but is sometimes called Tirfo-Thuinn – the land beneath the waves.

In the north-west you will find Loch Bhasapoll and a village called Baile nan Craganach (place of the clumsy people), so named because the villagers were thought to have six fingers on each hand. Still in the north, Dùn Mòr Vaul is a fine example of an Iron Age broch (dry-stone, hollow-walled structure) where artefacts from many ages have been found. The Ringing Stone, west of Vaul, is covered with pre-historic cup marks and emits an unearthly sound when struck. Strike carefully: it's said that Tiree will sink beneath the waves should the stone ever be broken.

To the south of the Isle of Skye lies the small archipelago known as the Small Isles, consisting of four main islands – Canna, Rum, Eigg and Muck – some smaller ones including Sanday and a number of skerries.

Sanday, usually viewed as one entity with Canna, is linked to its larger neighbour by sandbanks at low tide and a road bridge for the less adventurous. Like Canna, it is owned by the National Trust of Scotland and parts of the 184 hectare island are used for crofting. Ferries from Mallaig serve both islands. On entering the harbour one is confronted by a rockface covered with graffiti, originally the names of fishing boats and traders from the Baltic but now also including the names of attention-seeking visitors.

Canna is seven kilometres long and 1.5 kilometres at its widest point and is run as a farm by the NTS, having been gifted to the trust by the Gaelic folklorist John Lorne Campbell in 1981. The principal house on the island, Canna House, contains Campbell's archives. On the coast east of Canna's harbour is An Coroghon, a medieval prison tower built on the site of an ancient fort where an 18th century laird is said to have imprisoned his daughter in attempt to ward off the attentions of her lover. The attempt was unsuccessful, and the young man carried his beloved off to his home on Skye.

On the north side of Canna is the burial site known as Uaigh Righ Lochlainn (the grave of the king of Norway), and there is plenty more evidence of Viking habitation on both islands. More recent residents have included a burgeoning

ABOVE Perfect
for walkers –
the Rum Cuillin

population of brown rats, whose presence was a deterrent to the islands' birdlife. Following a cull, Canna was declared rat-free and bird populations, including that of Manx shearwaters, have recovered.

By far the largest of the Small Isles is Rum, lying to the south-east of Canna.

Covering more than 10,000 hectares and with a population in 2011 of 22, Rum went by the invented name of Rhum for a long period in the 20th century because its owner at the time, Sir George Bullough, a noted textile magnate, playboy and racehorse breeder, was uneasy about being associated with the alcoholic spirit. Sir George's widow sold the island to Scottish Natural Heritage in 1957 on the understanding that it was to be used as a nature reserve, and Rum's inhabitants are mostly employees of SNH.

Those residents live in and around the village of Kinloch on the east coast, an area that has been inhabited by humans for many millennia. Carbonised hazelnut shells found in Farm Fields, near Kinloch, have been dated to between 7700 and 7500BC, and a nearby beach site above Loch Scresort is thought to date back to between 6500 and 5500BC. This is evidence of some the earliest known human habitation of Scotland.

Construction of the Bulloughs' residence, the grand though rather dilapidated Kinloch Castle, began in 1897 and was completed in 1900. Remarkably, it was the first private residence in Scotland to be supplied with electricity. Kinloch is also the site of the ferry terminal, with services to and from Mallaig.

Rum's small population in relation to its size is due largely to its mountainous nature and its less than gentle climate. The island's range of hills, attractive to walkers, is known as the Rum Cuillin to distinguish it from Skye's better-known range, with which it shares geological characteristics.

Eigg (the name is pronounced 'egg' and is derived from The Gaelic for notch) lies to the south-east of Rum. This is an island of some 3,000 hectares, the second largest of the Small Isles, and a 2011 population of 83. It is also an island with an interesting recent history.

After many frustrating years of ownership by absentee landlords and countless unfulfilled promises, Eigg was bought in 1997 by the Isle of Eigg Heritage Trust, a partnership between the islanders, the Highland Council and the Scottish Wildlife Trust. The buyout, recorded in the book *Soil and Soul: People Versus Corporate Power* by Alastair McIntosh, has resulted in more responsible ownership and a growing population.

Visitors arrive by the Mallaig ferry at Galmisdale in the south-east but travel to Cleadale in the north-west to find the main centre of population. Here there is a quartz beach known as the singing sands because of the sound it makes when walked on. The island's centre takes the form of a moorland plateau with the extraordinary hump of Sgurr of Eigg rising to 393 metres above sea level. Views from the top of the Sgurr can be breathtaking.

Historic tales abound here. At Kildonnan are the ruins of a 14th century church built on the site of a seventh century monastery founded by Saint Donan. The saint and his 52 monks were slaughtered in 617, but the identity of the perpetrators is disputed. According to some it was a band of warrior women who lived on a crannog in Loch nam Ban Móra (loch of the mighty women); others says Norse pirates were responsible.

Muck, the smallest of the four main Small Isles, lies to the south of Eigg. This is a low-lying island of 560 hectares with a population of around 30 and a name thought to derive from the Gaelic for sea pig, or porpoise. It's known for its populations of this mammal and of seals.

Muck is normally a tranquil place but can be subject to mighty Atlantic storms. It is also a fertile island that is farmed by its owner and attracts enough visitors to keep the residents busy. Ferries arrive at Port Mor in the south-east, where there are camping facilities and a hotel.

Easily the largest of the Inner Hebrides at 165,000 hectares, Skye (or, to give it its Gaelic name, An t-Eilean Sgitheanach) is also the second largest of all of Scotland's islands after Lewis and Harris. The mountaineer Malcolm Slesser described the shape of Skye rather poetically as 'sticking out of the west coast of northern Scotland like a lobster's claw ready to snap at the fish bone of Harris and Lewis'.

The island is dominated by the dramatically jagged Cuillin mountain range, composed mainly of rough black igneous rock and basalt and rising at its highest point, Sgurr Alasdair, to 992 metres. The Black Cuillin – as opposed to the Red Cuillin, which are less rocky and lower – include no fewer than 12 Munros – mountains of over 3,000 feet. These present some of Scotland's most challenging hill walking and, in some cases, climbing skills that are far beyond the average visitor.

Skye's coastline is made up of a seemingly endless series of bays and peninsulas, and at an extremity of one of the latter lies the village of Kyleakin. It's here that most visitors will gain their first taste of the island thanks to the Skye Bridge, which spans the waters between Kyleakin and Kyle of Lochalsh on the mainland. The road bridge, which initially subjected drivers to a toll but is now free, was opened in 1995 to replace a popular ferry service.

ABOVE Dramatically jagged – the Cuillins, Isle of Skye

Driving up the east coast through Broadford – the location of Skye's airstrip – and continuing through the tortuous indentations of the coastline, one may perceive the outlying islands of Scalpay, Raasay and perhaps Rona.

The 25 square kilometre, heather-covered Scalpay gets its name from the Norse fondness for scallops, suggests one authority, and it offers holiday cottages and a shooting estate. Further out, Raasay (island of roe deer) has a population of over 150 within its 6,000 hectares and is famed as the birthplace of the poet Sorley

MacLean, sometimes viewed as the father of the Scottish Gaelic literary renaissance. Rona, sometimes called South Rona to distinguish it from its namesake far to the north, is 930 hectares of pure delight with a minuscule population but some of the oldest rocks in western Europe. The ruins of a 14th century chapel – perhaps originally a monk's cell – are to be found at the south end of the island.

Returning to Skye and continuing northwards, one will arrive at Portree, the largest settlement on the island and home to most of its services. Here you will find an attractive harbour and the Royal Hotel. Although some say the town has little of historical interest to offer, the hotel sits on the site of McNab's Inn, where Bonnie Prince Charlie is said to have bidden farewell to Flora MacDonald before fleeing to France in 1746.

North of Portree lies the Trotternish peninsula, which has basalt as its base and offers rich soils and stunning rock features. You will pass the Old Man of Storr, a 50 metre rock pillar that was first climbed in 1955. On the beach near Rigg is a rock shaped like a church where the Clan MacQueen is said to have invoked the devil by roasting cats. Equally fascinating is the Kilt Rock, a formation of black basalt with folded strata resembling tartan.

Still on the east side of the Trotternish peninsula, Staffin is said to be the site of a wreck of a galleon of the Spanish Armada in 1588. It is certainly the site of a small museum displaying a collection of dinosaur fossils and footprints. North of Staffin can be found the Quiraing, a wonderful series of spectacular rock formations. At the extreme northern tip of Trotternish lies Duntulm Castle, which was last occupied in 1732.

Descending the western side of Trotternish one is confronted by the sea wa-ters of Loch Snizort before arriving at the ferry port of Uig, which offers services to Harris and North Uist. Further south, one will turn north again at the village of Ske-abost – which has associations with Saint Columba – to explore the Waternish peninsula on Skye's north-west.

On its western side you may find the ruin of Trumpan Church, scene of one of the most murderous events in Scottish history. Here it was, in 1578, that the MacDonalds of Uist, intent on avenging a massacre, barricaded rival MacLeods in the church and set it on fire. All perished save for one girl. Gathering their remaining forces, the MacLeods set about the departing MacDonalds in their boats, slaying every last one.

The seat of the MacLeod clan is the fabulous Dunvegan Castle, accessed by the Fairy Bridge. This is the longest continuously inhabited castle in Scotland and has been in MacLeod hands since 1200.

Beyond Waternish to the west is the Duirinish peninsula, dominated by two peaks – Healabhal Bheag and Healabhal More – that are known as Macleod's Tables. The westernmost point of Skye is found at Neist Point, scene of a lighthouse and fantastic views.

Descending Skye's west coast by twists

and turns, one will eventually arrive at Carbost, where the island's famed malt whisky, Talisker, is distilled. Smooth, peaty and smoky, Talisker is perhaps an acquired taste, but it certainly appealed to the writer Robert Louis Stevenson, who opined: 'The king o' drinks, as I conceive it, Talisker, Islay, or Glenlivet.'

To the south of Carbost lie the majestic Black Cuillin with Sgurr Alasdair standing supreme. The mountain sits on the west side of Loch Coruisk, a freshwater loch just 10 metres above sea level that has been called one of the most awe-inspiring places on Earth. 'The Cauldron of Waters' is a deep, dark loch sitting within a natural amphitheatre of brooding mountains, accessible only by boat or after a 12-kilometre walk. It's worth the effort. Sir Walter Scott eulogised the loch thus: 'Rarely human eye has known / A scene so stern as that dread lake / With its dark ledge of barren stone …'

Offshore, to the west of Loch Scavaig, may be seen the island of Soay, home to the primitive breed of sheep of the same name. Indeed, the name comes from the Norse for 'sheep island'.

The most southerly point of Skye – the Point of Sleat on the peninsula of the same name – can be reached on foot.

The ruins of Dunscaith Castle, in legend the home of the Queen of Skye who taught the art of war to the Irish hero Cuchulainn, are on the west side of the peninsula. At Armadale, site of a ferry to Mallaig on the mainland, is the Clan Donald Centre, where the Museum of the Isles may be visited and visitors may stay in self-catering lodges.

Far to the north yet still counted among the Inner Hebrides, the Summer Isles – so named because they were used for summer grazing – cling to the Highland coast in the mouth of Loch Broom. They are not to be confused with Summerisle, the fictional island portrayed in the cult 1973 film *The Wicker Man*, which was actually filmed many miles south around Newton Stewart in Dumfries and Galloway. They do, however, crop up in an Ian R MacLeod novella that takes their name.

Tanera Mòr, the largest island of the archipelago at 310 hectares, is the also only one that is inhabited, boasting a population of four in 2011. It was the subject of Frank Fraser Darling's *Island Years*, published in 1940, which describes the experience of living on a small island. The 'large

island of the pasture' is composed of sandstone covered by peat and heather and is home to a salmon farm, a sailing school, holiday cottages and a post office, which is permitted to issue its own stamps.

In years gone by a fishing station of some importance, majoring on herring, was sited on the island. It's said that up to 200 fishing vessels at a time would anchor in The Anchorage, as Tanera Mòr's bay on the east coast is called, and salted herring would be exported as far as the Caribbean.

When fish stocks were scarce, however, the islanders of Tanera Mòr took enthusiastically to the illicit distilling of whisky, and another important economic development took place when the island was bought by a certain Captain MacDonald, who enjoyed a reputation as a talented smuggler. Local legend has it that a cargo

of rum is buried at Tigh-an-Quay, on the island's east coast, and that there is further treasure to be discovered between Tigh-an-Quay and the 122 metre Meall Mòr in the west.

The Summer Isles' waters also shelter Tanera Beag (Little Tanera, sitting within The Anchorage) and Bottle Island, so called because of its shape. More romantically named are Horse Island (confusingly, home only to a herd of goats) and Priest Island (said to have been an early Christian retreat and the refuge of a 'Popish' priest during the 28th century). Isle Martin, now a bird sanctuary, was once the site of a monastery established by the saint from whom the island takes its name. Isle Ristol, the innermost of the Summer Isles, is home to a Scottish Wildlife Trust reserve.

Chapter 4

The Outer Hebrides

The Western Isles – the name conjures up exotic images of far-flung lands reached after perilous journeys through treacherous waters. And while the truth is a little more prosaic, that vision is not *too* far from the reality.

The Outer Hebrides, to give the islands their more conventional name, are separated from the mainland of Scotland by roughly 70 kilometres of sometimes unfriendly waters. The 27,000 people of the 15 inhabited islands are also separated from the Scottish norm in other ways: over half of them, for example, speak Gaelic, and their industries still centre on crofting, fishing and weaving, far removed from the Silicon Glen of Scotland's central belt.

The Outer Hebrides – Na h'Eileanan Siar in Gaelic – stretch over 200 kilometres from Berneray in the south to the Butt of Lewis in the north, taking in more than 100 islands and skerries on the way. Small wonder that this archipelago was known collectively as the Long Isle in the olden days. Like their kin in the Inner Hebrides, the Western Isles enjoy a mild oceanic climate, benefiting from the warm waters of the Gulf Stream.

The Hebridean twins share much history, too. Stone Age and other prehistoric structures are scattered throughout the Western Isles, just as they are in the Inner Hebrides. After gaining the attention of various Roman and Greek authors – notably Pliny the Elder, who lived in the first century AD and referred to the 'Hebudes' in his encyclopaedic *Naturalis Historia* – the Hebrides became part of the king-

dom of the Norsemen in the ninth century. After 400 years of rule by men such as Ketill Flatnose, the Treaty of Perth in 1266 gave sovereignty to Scotland and the islands came effectively under the control of the chiefs of the great clans like the MacNeils, MacLeods and MacDonalds.

As in many another Scottish island chain, the 18th and 19th century Highland Clearances – known to the local people as Fuadach nan Gàidheal, the expulsion of the Gael – had a devastating effect on the Outer Hebrides. Much of Gaelic culture was destroyed and it is only recently that population declines have been reversed.

Happily for us and for the people of the Western Isles, much still remains of the culture, and it is now to be treasured for evermore. This is an island chain of immense charm, of mystery and of beauty; a chain that has embraced the modern era while never letting go of its past.

It is natural to start a journey through the Outer Hebrides at one extremity. Let us start in the south. Berneray, also known as Barra Head, was once Bjorn's Island. Not to be confused with the Berneray that lies off North Uist, it has an area of just over 200 hectares and has its highest point at Sotan (193 metres). Its last permanent inhabitants left around 1910.

Being at the southern end of the Outer Hebrides, Berneray is subject to the full fury of the Atlantic, and fish are sometimes found on top of the western cliffs after particularly strong gales. It's said that a storm in 1836 moved a 42 tonne rock almost two metres.

There are many prehistoric sites on the island, including four chambered tombs, five cists (stone-built coffin boxes), burial cairns and the supposed site of a chapel near MacLean's Point. Here an incised cross has been dated to between the sixth and ninth centuries. The Barra Head Lighthouse was built by the famous civil engineer Robert Stevenson and has been in operation since 1833.

Lying north of Berneray, the island of Mingulay hasn't been inhabited by man since 1912 but many birds still make it their home. Now in the keeping of the National Trust for Scotland, the island has important populations of razorbills, black-legged kittiwakes and puffins, which nest among sea cliffs that are among the highest in the British Isles.

A famous Mingulay story relates how a rent collector named Macphee was landed on the island but, finding every inhabitant dead, hurriedly warned the boatmen that there was 'plague' in the air. At this the panicking boatmen rowed away, leaving Macphee to his fate for an entire year. He survived, and today Macphee's Hill reminds us of his lonely wait.

Passing northwards from Mingulay you will pass Pabbay and Sandray before setting foot on Vatersay, a 960 hectare island with 90 inhabitants. This island, whose name has variously been translated as referring to water, fathers, priests and gloves, is the westernmost permanently inhabited place in Scotland. Vatersay is also the name of the island's only village.

The remains of an Iron Age broch are to be found Dun a' Chaolais in the north

THE OUTER HEBRIDES

and there is a Bronze Age cemetery at Treasabhaig, south of the island's highest point, the 190 metre Theiseabhal Mòr. The tiny islet of Biruaslum off the west coast features a walled fort thought to date from the Neolithic age.

Vatersay is nowadays linked to Barra to the north by a causeway completed in 1990. Before it was built, cattle on their way to market were obliged to swim across the Sound of Vatersay. The uproar following the drowning of an unfortunate prize bull by the name of Bernie in 1986 had the effect of speeding the causeway's construction.

Off the east coast lies a small island called Uinessan, where you may find the remains of the Chapel of Mary of the Heads. Mary was, it seems, an impatient woman who was wont to decapitate those who displeased her.

Barra, which Private Frazer often described as 'lonely' in the TV sitcom *Dad's Army*, is in fact rather more lively than he remembered. The population of more than 1,100 inhabit an island of nearly 6,000 hectares, with the main centre of habitation being the village of Castlebay. Named after the missionary Barr, a disciple of Saint Columba, Barra has a rocky and heavily indented east coast and sandy beaches on the west. A long coral reef lies at a depth of 100 metres off the coast.

The medieval castle of Kisimul stands on a small island off Castlebay. Sad to relate, Kisimul was abandoned in 1838 and some of its stones used for ballast in fishing boats, but it's in the safe hands of Historic Scotland now. Castlebay, at one time a prosperous herring port with 400 boats using its harbour, is today a busy place with hotels, shops and even a cottage hospital.

Spectacular views are to be gained from the two highest hills on Barra: Heaval (383 metres) and Ben Tangaval (333 metres). Walking to the peak of Heaval you will come across a white marble statue of the Madonna and child, erected in 1954. Other sites of interest on the island include a ruined church and museum at Cille Bharra, brochs at Dun Chuidhir and An Dun Ban and various other Iron Age structures.

A Hebridean island would not be complete without tales of the supernatural. In Barra there is a legend of an underground passage that runs between Cleat and Uaimh an Oir (cave of gold) on the east coast. The story goes that two hairless, mad dogs entered a cave at Cleat, emerging several days later at Uaimh an Oir. Their masters had entered the cave with them but were never seen again.

THE OUTER HEBRIDES

If you were to fly north from Barra, passing such deserted islands as Gighay and Hellisay on the way, you would see Eriskay nudging the south coast of South Uist – connected to it, in fact, by a causeway. This is an island with romantic associations strengthened by the exquisite strains of the old traditional song *The Eriskay Love Lilt*. One passage translates from the Gaelic:

> *When I'm lonely, dear white heart,*
> *Black the night and wild the sea,*
> *By love's light, my foot finds*
> *The old pathway to me.*

Eriskay is an island of 703 hectares and 150-ish inhabitants whose beauty lies more in its songs and other claims to fame than in its landscape. It was, for instance, the island that inspired the 1940s novel and film *Whisky Galore!*

In 1941 the cargo ship *SS Politician* was en route from Liverpool to the Caribbean, with 28,000 cases of malt whisky aboard, when she ran aground off Eriskay. The islanders seized the opportunity thus presented and salvaged the precious cargo for their own consumption, much to the outrage of the local customs officer. Some men, although innocent of anything other than opportunism in the eyes of local people, were charged and convicted of the crime of evading duty, and the ship was eventually blown up, leading one saddened islander to comment: 'Dynamiting whisky. You wouldn't think there'd be men in the world so crazy as that!'

There's more to Eriskay than whisky. Its name means goblin or water nymph island, and it's known for its Eriskay pony and its jersey, which is made without any seams.

South Uist is a larger island of 32,000 hectares and a population of 1,800. Like many islands in the Hebrides, it has a mountainous east coast – Beinn Mhòr rises to 620 metres – and a lower-lying, grassy coastal plain in the west; machair is the technical term. The spine of mountains is broken by three sea lochs and a fourth, Skiport, that slices through the island. The main population centre lies in Lochboisdale, from where ferries sail to Oban on the mainland and to Barra.

In the west, just north of Milton, may be found the birthplace of the Jacobite heroine Flora MacDonald, who helped Bonnie Prince Charlie evade capture after the disastrous Battle of Culloden in 1746. More history: the evidence that South Uist housed a Neolithic population of some importance is overpowering, and

THE OUTER HEBRIDES

the island is covered by sites of interest including the remains of chambered tombs, a Bronze Age hoard, brochs, roundhouses, Viking settlements, medieval longhouses and inscriptions in Ogham, the early medieval alphabet used to write the Gaelic languages of that time.

In 2002 at Cladh Hallan, near Daliburgh in the south-west, the mummified remains of a family were found under a Bronze Age roundhouse – the only deliberately mummified, prehistoric bodies to have been found in Britain. Tests showed that the bodies had been preserved in peatbog for between six and 18 months after their deaths between 1600 and 1300 BC, before being buried in about 1120BC. The reason for the delay in interment is not known.

On the island's east coast may be found Nicolson's Leap, and thereby hangs a tragic tale. The eponymous Nicolson, it's said, was found in bed with the wife of a clan chief. Escaping, he took the chief's baby son hostage and leapt a five-metre gap on to the rock stack. Nicolson's bargaining with his pursuers came to nought, and he eventually jumped to his death – and that of the baby – into the sea.

The island of Benbecula (little mountain of the fords) lies between the Uists North and South and is connected to both by causeways. Here the predominant religion changes from the Catholicism of the southerners (deasaich) to the Protestantism of the north.

Benbecula is also known to the poets among us as An t-Eilean Dorcha – the dark island. It's an isle of some 8,000 hectares and 1,300 residents, whose sole means of direct travel to the mainland is by air. Most of the land is low-lying and flat, with the solitary Rueval in the centre poking upwards to 124 metres. Some seagoing vessels have foundered in Benbecula's western waters, but because they are shallow, shipwrecked crews have often been able to wade ashore. It was from Benbecula that Bonnie Prince Charlie, with Flora MacDonald, sped 'over the sea to Skye'.

The island's airport is in the north-west. Just south of it is the main village, Balivanich, which translates as Town of the Monk and is the main administrative centre not only for Benbecula but also for North and South Uist. Here, also, are the headquarters for a deep sea artillery firing range, which is actually located on South Uist.

There is something of a puzzle surrounding the naming of Baleshare, which lies in the waters south-west of North Uist and north of Benbecula. The

LEFT Loch on North Uist

name means 'East Town', which leads one to suppose that there was once a West Town. And indeed there may have been before it was washed away by the waves in the 16th century.

Baleshare, which is linked to North Uist by a causeway, is the proud possessor of a fine, long sandy beach and home to around 60 residents. This 900-hectare island is remarkably flat, rising only to 12 metres at its highest point, and its archaeological sites are threatened by coastal erosion.

North Uist itself is also a low-lying place for the most part, with half of its area of 30 hectares under water, such is the profusion of lochs in some of which salmon and trout abound. Some of the lochs contain a mixture of salt and fresh water, making for unusual habitats. Loch Sgadabhagh – about which it has been said 'there is probably no other loch in Britain which approaches [it] in irregularity and complexity of outline ...' – has an area of eight square kilometres and a shoreline of 83 kilometres. But its neighbour, Loch Obisary, contains more than twice as much water.

More than 1,200 people make their homes on North Uist, mainly in the settlement of Lochmaddy (Loch of the Hounds), named after two dog-shaped rocks in the east-coast bay. The inhabitants of this place have to shake off a poor reputation earned in earlier times: a 1616 report declared that it was a 'rendezvous for pirates'. From here a ferry goes to Skye untroubled by buccaneers.

As you might justifiably expect of this part of the world, North Uist has a plethora of prehistoric structures, notably the Barpa Langais chambered cairn, the Pobull Fhinn stone circle, probably named after the ancient hero Fionn McCool, and standing stones at Na Fir Bhreige ('false men'). This, it is said, marks the graves of three traitors who were buried alive, although a rival tale contends that three men in question were turned to stone as punishment for having deserted their wives in Skye.

The islet of Eilean Dhomhnaill has been identified as possibly the earliest crannog, with pottery found there dating back to between 3200 and 2800BC. The site's turf-walled house and a timber screen surrounding them appear to have been taken down and rebuilt time after time.

The drastic effect of the Highland Clearances and mass emigration to Cape Breton is as marked on North Uist as anywhere. Emigration came as a result of the failure of the island's kelp industry in the

early 19th century; then the clearances contributed to the dwindling of the population. Before the clearances, the first of which took place in the 1820s, the population of the island had touched 5,000; by 1841 it had fallen to 3,870.

To the west of North Uist lie the Monach Islands, also known as Heisker ('bright skerry') and enjoying National Nature Reserve status that protects their birdlife, grey seal populations and machair. Uninhabited since 1947, the islands were formerly home to colonies of monks and nuns who gave them their name.

Of the five islands the main ones are Ceann Ear (the largest at 203 hectares), Ceann Iar and Shivinish, and they are all connected at low tide. It's thought that at one time it was possible to walk all the way from the Monachs to Baleshare and on to

North Uist eight kilometres away, but that the sandbanks were swept away by a massive tidal wave in 1607. It's possible that all three islands were linked at one time.

The remains of patches of grazing and cultivated land are still visible in a village in the south-west of Ceann Ear. The village was able to support a post office, a school and a missionary, but they are all long gone. In former times, monks and nuns were expected to keep a fire going on the western isle of Shillay in order to warn ships of treacherous rocks. Later, a red brick lighthouse was built and it has been succeeded by a solar-powered replacement.

Berneray – not to be confused with Barra Head, also known as Berneray, to the extreme south – sits on top of North Uist. There is evidence that it has been occupied by man since the Bronze Age, and possibly before. Nowadays, a population of about 150 inhabits its 1,000 hectares.

Both of the island's hills – the highest, Beinn Shléibhe (Moor Hill) tops out at 93 metres – are on the east side and the west has a four-kilometre white sand beach once described as one of the loveliest in Britain. Although Berneray lies close to North Uist, and although the population is concentrated in the south-east, it has traditionally been part of the parish of Harris.

The island is also known as the birthplace of Angus MacAskill, who was born in 1825 and grew to become the tallest natural (i.e. with no growth abnormalities) giant ever recorded. Having started life as an unremarkable baby, he emigrated with his family to Cape Breton in Canada and started to grow, eventually attaining a height of 2.35 metres (7ft 9in). MacAskill is remembered for his feats of strength such as lifting a fully grown horse over a fence.

Even Prince Charles has been to Berneray, living the life of a crofter for a week in the 1990s for a TV documentary. The prince lodged at the home of 'Splash' McKillop and his wife and, as the world's media wondered where he had disappeared to, took part in lobster fishing, potato digging (the island is known for its spuds) and tree planting. Some of the trees have even survived the worst the Atlantic can throw at them.

After passing across the Sound of Harris, having left behind islets and such various uninhabited islands as Ensay, Killegray and the beautiful little world of Pabbay, the last-named lying slightly to the west, you will land on Harris. Although it is often referred to as an island apart, it is joined to Lewis to the north by a sizeable chunk of land and the two are correctly referred to as Lewis and Harris.

This is Scotland's largest island at nearly 220,000 hectares. It is, indeed, the third largest island in the British Isles after Great Britain and Ireland. Together, Lewis and Harris had a population of more than 21,000 in 2011, which compared favourably with the 2001 total of nearly 20,000, but at one time in the 19th century more than 30,000 people inhabited the two islands – in those days the populations were counted separately.

A major industry here is the production of Harris tweed, which by law can only be made in the Outer Hebrides. It was kick-started by the wife of the Earl of Dunmore, a 19th century owner of Harris, who did much to popularise a fabric whose fame has spread worldwide.

Lewis and Harris are, or is, MacLeod territory. The clan has inhabited this part of the world since time immemorial and ruled the island from the 14th century, but more recent times have seen a multitude of owners, of parts and of the whole. The cleaning product industrialist and philanthropist William Lever, Lord Lev-

erhulme, bought both Lewis and Harris in 1918 and set about an attempt to develop the fishing industry, spending nearly a million pounds in the process. He gave the parish of Stornoway, the main town on the islands, to the local people and donated 41 crofts free of charge, but died in 1925, just as his plans were beginning to come to fruition. Leverhulme's executors abandoned his project and, having split the territory into several large estates, sold out. One of the results was mass emigration to North America.

Harris, the southern part of Lewis and Harris, is by far the junior partner in terms of size and population, with nearly 2,000 inhabitants in 2011. It, too, is divided into two parts – North and South Harris – where the sea lochs West and East Loch Tarbert almost meet at the main settlement of Tarbert (population 550), from where there are ferry connections to Skye. Tarbert also offers a hotel, shops selling the inevitable Harris tweed and a selection of eating places.

Harris's west coast features unspoilt sandy beaches and machair whose profusion of summer wild flowers is said to perfume the milk from the lucky cattle that graze there, while the east coast is more barren. Venture north of Tarbert

ABOVE Folded gneiss on Harris

and you will find a mountainous area whose highest point is found at Clisham, the Outer Hebrides' loftiest point at 799 metres. Here there are more than 30 peaks of more than 300 metres. South of Tarbert the landscape is less rugged and offers the aforementioned attractive beaches.

The road that winds southwards on the east coast of South Harris has been known as the Golden Road since it was built in 1897, and for good reason: it was extraordinarily expensive to construct. It reveals numerous small lochs, a landscape of browns and greys and a ragged coastline. Here the land is so unremittingly unforgiving and rocky that graves were hard to dig, and in past times the departed were taken to the west for burial. There are now very few inhabitants of the east, living or dead.

The Golden Road runs through the townships of Lickisto, Geocrab, Manish,

Flodabay, Ardvay, Finsbay and Lingerbay to arrive at Rodel, which has a neat little harbour and is surmounted by Saint Clement's Church. The church, built around 1500 by the eighth MacLeod, Alasdair the Hunchback, has a rectangular tower that is unique in the Outer Hebrides and encloses MacLeod's carved tomb.

North of Rodel, the township of Leverburgh is a reminder of Lord Leverhulme's efforts to bolster Harris's fortunes – here it was that he foresaw the centre of a mighty herring fishing industry. Nowadays a ferry links Leverburgh (Gaelic: An t-Ob; the haven) with Berneray and North Uist.

Perfect examples of the spectacular beaches mentioned earlier can be found at Tràigh an Taoibh Thuath (beach on the north side) and Tràigh Scarasta (beach/farm in the pass). The latter, as does Tràigh Seilebost, affords a view of the island of Taransay, the largest island without a permanent population in Scotland and the location for the filming of the BBC's *Castaway 2000*. This was a TV series in which 36 men, women and children were tasked with building a community.

At Paible on Taransay can be found two ancient chapels: one dedicated to Saint Taran, where only women were buried; the other to Saint Keith, where only men's remains were allowed. It's said that this arrangement was disrupted when a mixed burial took place in one of the graveyards, followed by the discovery the following morning of one of the bodies lying beside the grave.

Back on Harris, the A859 road turns inland and winds through a long valley on the way back to Tarbert, sitting on its neck of land (the name comes from the Gaelic for narrow isthmus). To the east, at the mouth of East Loch Tarbert, lies the island of Scalpay, also known as Scalpay of Harris to differentiate it from the island of the same name off Skye.

'Scallop Island' is an island of 653 hectares and a population of nearly 300 whose highest elevation is Beinn Scorabhaig at 104 metres. Four kilometres from top to bottom, Scalpay is connected to Harris by a 300 metre road bridge completed in 1998. Here the main industry is fish farming and prawn fishing. In 2013 the residents voted to accept the offer of the island's owner, English businessman Fred Taylor, and take over its running. The east coast of Scalpay is home to the Eilean Glas lighthouse, which was built in 1788 by the Commissioners of Northern Lights and was for a long time the only lighthouse in the Outer Hebrides.

The people of Scalpay – or Scalpachs, as they are known – enjoy a considerable reputation as sailors, and their skills were put to the test in 1962, when the trawler *Boston Heron* was driven on to rocks on the island's south coast. Six Scalpachs braved horrific conditions to launch a small open boat and rescue three trawlermen, one of whom was clinging to the rocks. Sadly, seven other trawler crew members lost their lives, but the Scalpachs' deeds were recognised with RNLI gallantry awards.

Back at Tarbert, continue on the A859 and you pass into North Harris, which is sparsely populated except by red deer, salmon and trout. You may find, on the shore of West Loch Tarbert, what is left of a whaling station that was built by Norwegians before World War I, only to be abandoned in 1930. The mountain of Clisham, accessible from the highest point on the road, offers walkers a challenging expedition that takes in several summits and is known as the Clisham Horseshoe.

As the road passes Loch Meavaig 13 kilometres north-west of Tarbert, you will come across Amhuinnsuidhe Castle, built by the Earl of Dunmore in 1868. June and July are the months to watch salmon leap stepped falls between sea and Loch Leosaid, and it was at the mansion that the author and dramatist JM Barrie, creator of *Peter Pan*, wrote his drama *Mary Rose*, which also treats the subject of an ageless child.

On the west coast of North Harris, at the end of a 20 kilometre single-track road, sits the idyllic, tiny settlement of Hushinish with its glorious bay and views of the uninhabited island of Scarp. This island was the scene of extraordinary attempts by the German inventor Gerhard Zucker to deliver mail by rocket in 1934. His experiments were unsuccessful – due, it's said, to Zucker's inability to obtain the correct fuel – and the resultant singed envelopes can now be seen at the Museum nan Eilean in Stornoway.

Harris is separated from Lewis by a natural 10 kilometre barrier in the shape of mountains and moorland between the sea lochs of Seaforth and Erisort. The two 'islands' that make up the whole are also separated by different Gaelic dialects and have always been considered distinct isles.

Compared with its southern neighbour, Lewis is comparatively flat except for its southern part. Here Mealisval (574 metres, in the west) and Beinn Mhor (572 metres, in the east) achieve supremacy over 16 other peaks of over 300 metres. The lower, flatter landscape has proved

ABOVE Callanish
standing stones, Lewis

more welcoming to man, and the main settlement on Lewis and Harris, Stornoway, boasts a population of 9,000 out of a total on Lewis of 19,000.

Stornoway is the third largest town in the Highlands area of Scotland after Inverness and Fort William. It was founded by Vikings in the ninth century, under the name of Stjórnavágr, around a natural, sheltered harbour and today is the centre of a fishing industry that is, however, much reduced from its 19th century heyday. Ferries run from Stornoway to Ullapool on the Scottish mainland and there are regular flights to Scotland's major cities, but there has been recent talk of a submarine tunnel linking Lewis and the mainland. If it is ever built it will be, at 65

66   ISLANDS OF SCOTLAND

kilometres, the world's longest road tunnel by some distance.

Stornoway's oldest building might be an 18th century net loft on North Beach Quay, although St Peter's Episcopal Church boasts an ancient sandstone font that was fetched over from the Hermit's Chapel on the Flannan Isles, more than 30 kilometres to the west. The church's Tower Bell dates back to 1631 and in the vestry can be found the explorer David Livingstone's 1608 Bible. Despite this antiquity and its remoteness from the centres of European civilisation, Stornoway is a modern place whose bustling streets come as quite a surprise to some visitors.

Another centre of population is to be found in the Eye Peninsula to its east. On the north shore of the isthmus connecting Eye and Stornoway is a 14th century church whose graveyard contains the bones of 19 MacLeod chiefs. From the other side of the town, roads head westwards towards Loch Roag and northwest, across moorlands, to Barvas. This is prime peat-cutting territory where hundreds of tiny lochs pit the landscape. One of Europe's best salmon rivers can be found at Abhainn Grimersta, and here you are not far from the lobster fishing island of Great Bernera, which lies in Loch Roag and is accessible by a road bridge.

Around 250 souls inhabit this island of over 2,000 hectares, and its people haven't always been able to live peaceful lives. Great Bernera is known for a riot, in response to the Highland Clearances, that shook Scotland in 1874. This resulted in the first successful legal challenge to landlordism in the Highlands and Islands and paved the way for land reform. Another violent occurrence was averted when the first pre-stressed concrete bridge was built in 1953 to connect the island to Lewis. Its construction came as a result of the islanders threatening to blow up a hillside to form a causeway.

Great Bernera has further historic treasures to offer. One is the semicircle of standing stones facing across the strait to Lewis and known as Callanish VIII, with the ruins of Dun Barraglom broch nearby. Another is an Iron Age, perhaps Pictish, settlement at Bostadh, discovered in 1992 and now covered with sand in order to preserve it. A replica Iron Age house nearby gives an idea of what lies beneath the sand.

Back on Lewis, travelling west to the bay of Uig will bring you to the scene of a truly remarkable discovery. In 1831, in dunes behind the beach, 78 chess pieces carved from walrus ivory and whales' teeth in the 12th century were uncovered – but stories of the chessmen's discovery vary. Some say it was a cow that exposed the trove, but the generally accepted version is that Malcolm 'Sport' MacLeod was the true discoverer. He exhibited the priceless pieces in his byre before selling them on. They are now to be seen in the British Museum and the National Museum of Scotland.

Some authorities suggest the chessmen were hidden or lost while they were being transported from their place of manufacture in Norway to Ireland. Whatever actually happened, a more stunning setting could not have been chosen for their disappearance – the sands of Uig have been described as framing one of the most beautiful views in Scotland: a virginal white beach, an indigo to viridian sea and purple heather-covered hills behind.

The road from Stornoway reaches one of Britain's most important and impressive archaeological sites at Callanish, at the head of East Loch Roag. The Callanish standing stones are older than both Stonehenge and the Pyramids, having been erected between 2900 and 2600BC, though it's possible that there were buildings on the site even earlier.

Thirteen primary stones form a circle with a diameter of 13 metres, and there is a long approach avenue of further stones to the north and shorter rows to the east, south and west. The stones, which are of the local Lewisian gneiss, vary from around one to five metres in height and the tallest marks the entrance to a burial cairn in which human remains have been found. Local legend has it that Saint Kieran, one of the Twelve Apostles of Ireland, tried to convert giants living on the island to Christianity and, faced with their refusal, turned them to stone.

Also on the west coast, overlooking Loch Carloway, is one of the best preserved brochs in Scotland. Dun Carloway, probably built in the first century AD and used for centuries as a stronghold, is 15 metres in diameter and parts of its east wall remain about nine metres high. Also near the village of Carloway, the crofting township of Garenin has the last remaining street of 'black houses' on the island of Lewis. Nine traditional thatched cottages have been preserved and restored, and the site offers tourist facilities.

Black houses, with walls up to two metres thick and thatch and turf roofs weighted down with stones, were built to withstand anything the Hebridean climate could throw at them. Animals lived alongside humans and peat fires burned despite the lack of a chimney in these fascinating structures. Visitors can experience their cosiness for themselves at the Blackhouse Museum, run by Historic Scotland, at Arnol, further up the west coast from Carloway.

As you move northwards you may come across further prehistoric sites including brochs, duns and the ruins of temples, of which more anon. One example is the tallest standing stone in Scotland, nearly six metres high, which is to be found at Ballantrushal. The Clach an Trushal ('Stone of Compassion') is believed by some to mark the site of a great battle, but it's more likely that it's all that remains of a stone circle built over 5,000 years ago.

The road north ends at Port of Ness, and it's from here that 10 men of Lewis sail 65 kilometres north every August to the tiny island of Sula Sgeir. Their mission? To perch precariously on vertiginous cliffs, sometimes for several weeks, and get their hands on up to 2,000 plump guga (young gannet) chicks. The birds are taken from their nests, plucked, quartered and salted for transport back to Lewis, where they are considered a delicacy. Animal welfare campaigners are scathing in their condemnation of the practice, and

some observers are equally critical of the taste of the strongly flavoured guga.

A little to the north of Port of Ness, on an inter-tidal sea stack, is the fort of Dun Eistean, the historical stronghold of Clan Morrison. Indeed, a bridge was built in 2002 to allow the clan to hold gatherings there.

The most northerly settlement on Lewis is Eoropie (from the Old Norse for beach village) and near here is the 'pygmy's isle'. Luchruban or Eilean nan Daoine Beaga (isle of the little people) is reputed to have been home to a pygmy tribe said to have their 'ane little kirk (church) in it of their ane handey wark'. Disappointingly, although an excavation of the church did indeed reveal many small bones, they were later found to be those of non-human animals.

Almost as far north as you can go on Lewis without toppling into the sea is the restored Teampull Mhoulaidh – Saint Moluag's Church. This is a 13th century building, dedicated to the saint and reputedly built by the son of a Scandinavian king who had converted to Christianity, with an engaging history. It gained a reputation as a place of healing, especially effective for those with mental afflictions, and sufferers who could not travel to the

THE OUTER HEBRIDES

church in person often availed themselves of an unusual solution: they would send wooden reproductions of their wounds or sores for the saint to deal with.

About a kilometre and a half to the north of Eoropie, one arrives at the Butt of Lewis, where spectacular cliffs brood over often tempestuous seas and an arresting redbrick lighthouse guides shipping on its way. After that, it's a long, long way to Sula Sgeir, the equally remote island of Rona and, eventually, the Faeroe Islands, more than 300 kilometres to the north.

But one cannot possibly leave Lewis and Harris without contemplating the mysteries of the Shiant Isles, off the south-east coast of Lewis. These – Garbh Eilean (rough island), Eilean an Tigh (home island) and Eilean Mhuire (island of Mary) – are, according to their name, the enchanted islands.

They are one of very few places where *Rattus rattus*, the black rat, can still be found in the UK; they were also found to be the home of the oldest puffin, of a venerable 34 years, ever discovered in these islands. And the sound between the Shiant Islands is traditionally the haunt of the Blue Men of the Minch, who are likely to drag you to the seabed if you fail to answer their questions in Gaelic rhyming couplets.

Chapter 5

Orkney

If you were able to jump in a light aircraft and fly north-east from Scotland's most northerly point, Easter Head on the Dunnet Head peninsula, you would first espy Stroma and Swona, uninhabited islands in the Pentland Firth away to your right, and then the archipelago known as Orkney. Lying 16 kilometres north of Caithness, the chain – never call it the Orkney Islands; it's simply Orkney – consists of around 70 islands on which humans have lived for at least 8,500 years. Twenty islands are still inhabited, making up a population of 21,000 at the time of the last census in 2011.

The isles of Orkney are fertile places where agriculture is the major contributor to the economy but where the strength of the tides and winds make alternative means of energy generation increasingly important. Orcadians, as Orkney's people are known, speak a dialect of Scots that contains hints of an extinct Germanic language, Norn, and has links to Shetlandic, spoken even further north.

The largest island in the chain, known simply as the Mainland, is the sixth largest of Scotland's islands at more than 52,000 hectares. More than three quarters of Orkney's inhabitants live on Mainland and the rest of the population is far-flung; the chain measures 80 kilometres from south-west to north-east and covers an area of 975 square kilometres.

These are mainly low-lying islands, although some western cliffs rise abruptly from the sea and there are enough sandstone hills on Mainland, Hoy and Rousay

ABOVE Tomb of
the Eagles, South
Ronaldsay, Orkney

to keep climbers interested. Lochs dot
the islands' surfaces and the coastlines
are, as is common in the islands of Scotland, pleasingly jagged. Mariners beware:
treacherous tidal currents – roosts, as
they're called by local people – and whirlpools swirl about these islands.

Orkney is justly famed for its wildlife.
Colonies of seabirds like puffins, guillemots, skuas and kittiwakes abound and

the mammal life includes grey and common seals, otters, dolphins and whales
and, at the other end of the size scale, the
Orkney vole. This is a distinct sub-species
of the common vole and can be found
nowhere else.

On the islands of Orkney you will find
some of the oldest Neolithic sites in Europe, some of them in superb states of
preservation. One group of monuments

on Mainland, known as the Heart of Neolithic Orkney, has been designated a UNESCO World Heritage Site. There are reminders, too, of the islands' Pictish era, and of their invasion and settlement by the Norsemen in the ninth century. They were only returned to the Scottish Crown in 1472, following the non-payment of a dowry for Margaret of Denmark, the bride of James III.

There are few excuses for failing to visit Orkney. They can be reached by ferry and air, and there are numerous ferry services between the islands. Here you can even find the world's shortest scheduled air service – the flight between Westray and Papa Westray can take less than a minute if the wind is in the right direction.

While Orkney is within easy reach, it can sometimes seem a world apart.

The most southerly inhabited island of Orkney is South Ronaldsay, which is linked to Mainland but has no such connections with its near namesake North Ronaldsay, which lies at the northern extreme of the archipelago. The links are courtesy of the Churchill Barriers, a series of four causeways that connect Mainland to South Ron-aldsay via Burray and the smaller islands of Lamb Holm and Glims Holm.

World War II had been in progress a mere month in October 1939 when a German U-boat slipped past the defences of Scapa Flow, where Viking ships had once anchored but was at that time the UK's chief naval base, and torpedoed *HMS Royal Oak* at her moorings, with the loss of 833 crewmen. In a bid to prevent further attacks, the First Lord of the Admiralty, Winston Churchill, ordered the building of four permanent barriers, but they were only completed in September 1944 and officially opened after the war had ended.

South Ronaldsay's name, like most in Orkney, comes from the Old Norse and means Rognvald's, or Ronald's, island. It's an island of nearly 5,000 hectares, making it the fourth largest in Orkney, and a population of nearly 1,000. The third largest settlement in these islands, St Margaret's Hope, is at the north of the island, from where ferries sail to Gills Bay, west of John O'Groats on the Scottish mainland. Some people claim the village is named after Margaret, Maid of Norway, an heiress to the Scottish throne who died at the age of seven in 1290. It's more likely that it commemorates the second wife of Malcolm III, king of the 11th century.

It was here that in 1263 King Haakon of Norway anchored his fleet of 120 ships – the largest to enter Scapa Flow before the 20th century – at the time of an eclipse of the sun. Some people say the eclipse was an omen of the disastrous Battle of Largs. Three years later, Haakon's successor Magnus signed the Treaty of Perth, which ceded sovereignty of the Western Isles to the Scottish Crown.

St Margaret's Hope, which features a blacksmith's museum, is also known hereabouts for its annual ploughing match, in which young boys plough in the nearby Sand of Wright, with girls dressed in dark jackets playing the part of the horses.

To the west of St Margaret's Hope is the Hoxa peninsula, where there is the site of a broch said to be where Thorfinn Torf-Einarsson, also known as Skullsplitter, Earl of Orkney in the 10th century, is buried. He appears in the *Orkneyinga Saga*, a narrative of the history of Orkney written around 1230 which, it is said, has no parallel in the social and literary record of Scotland.

South Ronaldsay's highest point (118 metres) is further south at Ward Hill, and in the south-east of the island is the 5,000-year-old chambered cairn known as the Tomb of the Eagles. Here, in 1958, were discovered around 16,000 human bones together with the remains of a number of white-tailed sea eagles. Evidence suggests that the human remains had been exposed to the elements to remove the flesh before being buried. The site, which seems to have been used continuously for 1,000 years or more, benefits from a museum in which ancient artefacts can be handled.

Crossing Churchill Barrier 4 will bring you to the island of Burray (broch island). This is an island of 900 hectares with a 2011 population of 409 whose main settlement is Burray Village, a former fishing port in the south-west.

Burray's history contains the exploits of the 18th century laird Sir James Stewart, who was involved with a murder on Mainland in 1725 and went on the run for 20 years before turning up at the Battle of Culloden. Surviving the battle, he thought it safe to return home to Burray but there he was confronted by a son of the murder victim, who turned him over to the authorities. Stewart ended his days in a London prison.

In order to travel from Burray to Mainland, cross the Churchill Barriers 3, 2 and 1, taking you via the uninhabited Gilms Holm and Lamb Holm, but you may want to linger a while on the

latter islet. Its most notable feature is a remarkably ornamented chapel built by Italian prisoners of war – the same men who constructed the Churchill Barriers – during World War II. The prisoners, who had been captured in North Africa, set about converting two Nissen huts into a structure that captivates. It is lined with plasterwork, has an altar made out of concrete and one end painted by the workers' leader, Domenico Chiocchetti. The chapel's front façade was fashioned out of concrete to hide the shape of the hut beneath. Signor Chiocchetti and others returned in 1960 to restore the paintings and interior to their former glory, and their work can still be admired by churchgoers and visitors.

As you pass on to Mainland, you may glimpse the isle of Copinsay (seal pup is-

ABOVE Italian Chapel on Lamb Holm, Orkney, built by prisoners of war

land) away to the east. This is the home of the fabled Copinsay Brownie, a kindly spirit from the depths of the sea whose good and faithful work for a farmer came to an end when the latter's new wife, embarrassed by the brownie's nakedness, made him a cloak. It seems the idea of clothing upset poor Hughbo, who fled into the night and was never seen again.

Off the north-eastern tip of the island lies the Horse of Copinsay, a stack of rock 18 metres high where once sheep and pigs were grazed. Nowadays it is remarkable for a hole through which water is blasted 60 metres into the air when an easterly gale stirs the waters.

Copinsay lies off the Mainland's eastern peninsula of Deerness. This was a Norse hunting ground where the bones of red deer can still be found in the peat bogs. If you are inclined towards a short walk at the Brough of Deerness, you may discover the ruins of an ancient monastery, the object of pilgrimages until the 17th century. Here pilgrims would walk round the building chanting and casting holy water and stones behind them.

An alternative name for Mainland in Norse times was Hrossey, which translates as Horse Island. There was also a time when it was referred to by a few peo-

LEFT Cathedral of Saint Magnus, Kirkwall, Orkney

ple as Pomona, the result of a mistranslation by the 16th century historian George Buchanan, but we should be thankful that the name did not stick.

Passing Mainland's airport as you travel west from Deerness, you will arrive at Kirkwall, the biggest town in Orkney and home to around 8,500 people. The town was mentioned in the *Orkneyinga Saga* as being the residence in 1046 of the Earl of Orkney Rognvald Brusason, who met his death at the hands of Thorfinn the Mighty. The latter is said to have been the most powerful of all the earls who ruled nine earldoms in Scotland and Ireland and was in power in Orkney for no fewer than 75 years.

Kirkwall, whose name comes from the Norse for Church Bay, was granted a royal charter and elevated to the status of a royal burgh by James III of Scotland in 1486, and modern roadsigns still indicate that you are entering royal territory. The town stands on the narrow isthmus that separates east and west Mainland.

Kirkwall's Cathedral of St Magnus dominates the town's skyline. The most northerly cathedral in the British Isles, it is not owned by any church (although it is a parish church of the Church of Scotland) but by the burgh and, uniquely for a British cathedral, has its own dungeon.

Construction was started in 1137 by Rognvald III, nephew of Saint Magnus who was martyred in 1117 and buried at Birsay in the north-west corner of Mainland. Building continued for 300 years and the cathedral was saved from destruction during the Reformation by the people of the town. When, later, the forces of Oliver Cromwell arrived they used it as a prison and stable. After that the building deteriorated, but it was restored between 1913 and 1930 and again during the 1989s.

The dungeon is known as Marwick's Hole; no one really knows why. Among the stories told about it is the tale of a 17th century woman, Jane Forsyth, who was sentenced to death by burning after being found guilty of witchcraft. Her lover helped her to escape the dungeon and the couple fled to Manchester.

Near the cathedral is the Bishop's Palace, which was built at the same time for William the Old, a 12th century bishop of Orkney. It was here that Haakon IV of Norway spent the winter following his defeat in the Battle of Largs in 1263, and it was here that he died, marking the end of Norse Rule over the Western Isles. The palace was restored after 1540 by Bishop Robert Reid, the founder of Edinburgh University.

Opposite the Bishop's Palace is the 17th

ABOVE Brig o'
Waithe, Stenness,
Mainland, Orkney

century Earl's Palace, considered by some to be the finest building of its era in Scotland. It was built by forced labour on the orders of the brutal Patrick Stewart, second Earl of Orkney, who was known as Black Pate. Proving that evil will never triumph, Stewart was later beheaded for treason.

Kirkwall is full of attractive reminders of history – including many 17th and 18th century houses – but one no longer exists: the town's medieval castle was destroyed in the 1600s. But on the western edge of the town is the prehistoric Grain Earth House, a low, stone-walled passage leading underground to a pillared chamber. This, and the Rennibister Earth House further west, are examples of the subterranean house of the Iron Age, once common in these islands and in Ireland. It was once connected to a surface dwelling, of which nothing remains, and is now in the care of Historic Scotland.

Kirkwall's Ba Game is an example of a fine old tradition maintained. One of a number of football games still played in the streets and fields of Britain, it dates back to the mid-17th century and has traditionally pitted people of the two halves of the town – the Uppies and the Doonies – against each other, but nowadays players

are drawn from all parts of Orkney. There are games for children, women and men but the goals are the same: the sea for the Doonies (the ball must be immersed in Kirkwall Bay) and the Lang, at the junction of Main Street with New Scapa Road, for the Uppies.

In the men's game, the ball (Ba') is thrown up at the Merket Cross when the cathedral bell strikes 13. It then disappears into a scrum of up to 350 men and the play surges back and forth, in wide and narrow streets, until a goal is reached. The rules are few but play is generally good-natured, if boisterous.

A more restrained leisure activity in Kirkwall comes in the form of a visit to the Orkney Museum, which tells the story of the archipelago from the Stone Age to the present day. The building in which it is sited, Tankerness House, was for three centuries the home of the Baikie family of the Tankerness peninsula about 12 kilometres south-east of Kirkwall. This was a family of merchants descended from the navigator of Haakon IV of Norway who took over the pre-Reformation house in 1641. Now A-Listed, the house's library and drawing room give an idea of how it looked when it was a family home.

The other museum in Kirkwall holds equal fascination for the visitor, albeit on a smaller scale. The Orkney Wireless Museum displays a collection of domestic and military equipment and marks the importance of wireless communications in Orkney during World War II.

Most of Mainland lies to the west of Kirkwall. Drive south-westwards from the town and you will pass the shores of Scapa Flow and through the Hobbister Hill, a Royal Society for the Protection of Birds reserve that is a mixture of sea cliffs, saltmarsh, sand flats and moorland. In the moors you may be lucky enough the see hen harriers, short-eared owls or red-throated divers, while at the coast there's a chance to spot red-breasted mergansers and black guillemots.

A little further west is the location for creature-spotting of a less certain kind. In Swanbister Bay lurks – or lurked, at least according to excited observers in the 1830s – a sea monster, or perhaps two, bearing a resemblance to that which inhabits Loch Ness, many miles to the south-west.

North of Swanbister is the highest peak on Mainland, Mid Hill, which attains a height of 271 metres. To the east of the hill was fought the last pitched battle on Orkney, as recently as 1529. In that year

LEFT Loch of Skaill, Mainland, Orkney

ABOVE Ring of Brodgar, Mainland, Orkney

William Sinclair, in trying to seize control of the earldom from his uncle, raised a force of 500 men with the help of the Earl of Caithness and landed on Mainland on the north side of Scapa Flow, to meet a large number of Orcadians in battle.

According to legend, when the Earl of Caithness landed with his men, a witch walked before them as they marched. She unwound two balls of wool – one blue, the other red – and found that the red ball ran out first, leading her to assure the earl that the side whose blood was spilled first would be defeated. The earl therefore determined to kill the first Orcadian he met, who happened to be a herd boy. Once the defenceless youth had been slain, the witch revealed that he was no Orcadian but a lad from Caithness who had taken refuge on Orkney. The invading force, unnerved by the incident, was routed in the ensuing battle.

There are more tales of murder to be found on Mainland, and one is centred on nearby Orphir Bay. It was here that the killer of Saint Magnus, Earl Haakon Paulson, built a small church. One authority, Hamish Haswell-Smith, speculates that Paulson must have done penance for the murder by going on a pilgrimage or crusade to the Holy Land, for the church's design is similar to that of the Holy Sepulchre in Jerusalem.

North of Mid Hill, in an island crowded with prehistoric sites, is one of the most remarkable you will ever see. This is the place UNESCO designated as a World Heritage Site: the Heart of Neolithic Orkney. Known to those in the know as HONO for short, this is an extraordinary collection of domestic and ritual monuments constructed around 5,000 years ago. Historic Scotland, which manages the sites, says that individually the sites are masterpieces of Neolithic design and construction, but collectively they represent one of the richest surviving Neolithic landscapes in western Europe, and give exceptional insights into the society, skills and spiritual beliefs of the people who constructed them. That is a more than adequate description of sites that attract thousands of visitors year after year.

It was a century and a half ago, in 1850, that a violent storm that claimed more than 200 lives ripped the earth from a large knoll beside the west-coast Bay of Skaill, known to the local people as Skerrabra. When the storm had abated and the villagers investigated, they found the outline of a village containing roofless houses. Attempts at excavation were made, but it wasn't until 1924, when another storm destroyed part of one of the houses, that the decision was made to protect and investigate more fully the settlement that is known today as Skara Brae. It has been hailed as the best preserved group of Neolithic houses in western Europe.

The houses, built from closely fitting flat stone slabs set into large mounds of household refuse, or midden, were linked

ORKNEY

RIGHT Streets
of Stromness,
Mainland, Orkney

by covered passages. Each house consisted of a single room with a floor space of around 40 square metres. The stone furniture in the room consisted of a dresser – perhaps for the storage and display of prized objects – two box beds, a central hearth and small tanks set into the floor. It has been speculated that these were perhaps used for the preparation of fish bait.

Archaeological digs have uncovered a range of artefacts, including dice used for gaming, hand tools, pottery and jewellery such as necklaces, beads, pendants and pins. Beautifully carved stone objects, perhaps used in religious rituals, have also been found, proving that the villagers – farmers, hunters and fishermen – were capable of producing things of sophistication with basic technology. This seems to have been a peaceful settlement, for no weapons have been found. Today's visitors to Skara Brae may view a replica construction of a house and take a look at most of the artefacts in the visitor centre.

Life in Skara Brae seems to have come to an end around 2500BC – no one knows why. At that time, other monuments were coming into being on Orkney, including a chambered tomb at Maeshowe and the nearby stone circles of Stenness and Brodgar.

At the south-east corner of the Loch of Stenness, Maeshowe is described as the finest Neolithic building in north-west Europe. Its use of massive individual stones marks it out as a masterpiece of design and construction, particularly when one remembers that its creators were working without metal tools or powered machinery. It is simply not to be missed.

From the outside, Maeshowe appears simply to be a large, grassy mound – the word 'howe' derives from the Old Norse for a hill. But enter by the only doorway, stoop to walk along a long stone passage and emerge into a central, stone-built chamber and that impression, along with the sunlight, is left far behind. The chamber is just 4.7 metres across but everything else is on a monumental scale. Each wall of the 10-metre passage is formed from a single, enormous sandstone slab, up to three tonnes in weight. The central chamber has a huge upright standing stone at each corner and off to the sides are three cells whose floors, back walls and ceilings are, again, single stone slabs.

This is a mysterious place, but some things are certain. The gently sloping passage was aligned with the utmost care, so that at sunset during the three weeks before and after midwinter, on December

21, sunlight shines down the passage to illuminate the back of the central chamber. The sun's rays align with a standing stone, the Barnhouse Stone, standing 800 metres south-south-west of Maeshowe.

The site was used for several hundred years as a burial tomb before being closed up. Three thousand years later, Norsemen broke into the mound and left behind graffiti in the form of runes of a light-hearted nature – the largest collection of surviving runic inscription outside Scandinavia.

Just to the south of Maeshowe stand the Stones of Stenness ('promontory of stones'), one of two henge monuments in the Heart of Neolithic Orkney. Indeed, these particular stones may form the earliest henge monument in the British Isles, dating from around 5,400 years ago. Archaeologists believe that, like the Ring of Brodgar, the site was used for activities and ceremonies celebrating the relationship between living and past communities.

The henge itself was a substantial ditch and outer bank, forming a physical obstacle around the circle of standing stones. The only way into and out of the circle was via causeways – there were two at Brodgar and one at Stenness.

The site was once encircled by a ditch and bank; digs have shown the ditch to be four metres wide and 2.3 metres deep. The four surviving standing stones, stone stumps and concrete markers outline an oval that was approximately 30 metres across.

The focus of the ring's interior, a large hearth, is still visible. The hearth's significance can be gauged from the line of features that marked the approach to it – a paved path, two stone settings, another setting that was apparently a second hearth, and the uprights of a three-stone dolmen (a tomb with a large flat stone laid on upright ones). Pottery and animal bones recovered from digs tell us that Neolithic people cooked and ate plenty at the site.

Just 1.5 kilometres north of Stenness, on a narrow isthmus between Loch Harray (where up to 10,000 duck pass the winter) and Loch Stenness, is the Ring of Brodgar, of whose 60 original stones 36 survive. The 19th century geologist Hugh Miller described the stones as resembling 'an assemblage of ancient druids, mysteriously stern and invincibly silent and shaggy'. The ring is indeed an impressive sight.

It forms an almost perfect circle, unlike the Stones of Stenness, and is one of the largest Neolithic henge monuments, measuring 130 metres in diameter overall. The ring of stones in itself has a diameter of 104 metres. There are two causeways crossing the ditch, which was originally 10 metres wide and 3.4 metres deep.

The Ring of Brodgar is yet to yield all of its secrets as the interior has not yet been excavated fully and the site's significance is not completely understood. While we await some kind of confirmation, we can estimate that the Ring was built between 2500 and 2000BC.

Not part of the Heart of Neolithic Orkney but fascinating nonetheless, Unstain Cairn can be found where Loch Stenness meets the sea. This chambered cairn was first excavated in 1844 and yielded the largest collection of Stone Age pottery ever found in Scotland – now housed in the Royal Scottish Museum in Edinburgh – and two seated skeletons.

These prehistoric sites will always be the subject of speculation, and some aspects of their later history have also thrown up some interesting theories. It's thought by some people, for example, that when Scandinavians reached Orkney in the ninth century they brought with them their pantheon of gods and other spiritual beliefs, and imposed them on the ancient monuments they found. Perhaps, then, the Ring of Brodgar and the Stones of Stenness really were known as the Temple of the Sun and Moon, and

LEFT The Old Man of Hoy sea stack, Orkney

perhaps young people really did make vows and pray to Odin here. True or not, we are allowed to dream.

Stromness, a parish and a town in south-west Mainland, is Orkney's second largest centre of population with more than 2,000 inhabitants and a long-established seaport. This town, whose name means 'headland protruding into the tidal stream', can be reached by ferry from Scrabster on the Scottish mainland and is well worth exploring for a few hours.

Its winding main street is filled by houses and shops made from local stone and has many a narrow lane branching off it. The town was recorded as the site of an inn in the 16th century and grew in importance in the late 1600s, when war with France meant shipping was well advised to avoid the English Channel. From 1670 to 1891 Stromness was a base for the Hudson's Bay Company (North America's oldest commercial corporation) and later it served as a port for the Davis Strait whaling fleet. The ships of Captain Cook, after his Pacific expedition, and Sir John Franklin, before his voyage to find the North-West Passage, were serviced here.

Stromness Museum displays aspects of the town's whaling history, including Inuit artefacts brought back as souvenirs from Greenland and Arctic Canada. Other reminders of the whaling past come in the form of displays of whalebones on many of the town's buildings.

Stromness has long had international connections, and these persist today in the form of the European Marine Energy Centre. This important hub is the only centre of its kind in the world and offers developers of wave and tidal energy devices the opportunity to test their products. A number of renewables companies have set up in Stromness since the centre was opened in 2003.

Travel up Mainland's west coast from Stromness, past Skara Brae, and you will come to Marwick Head, the scene of a dramatic historical event of the 20th century. In 1916 the senior Army officer Field Marshall Kitchener, while aboard the armoured cruiser *HMS Hampshire* en route to Russia on a diplomatic mission, was killed when the ship hit a mine laid by a German U-boat and sank. Kitchener was just one of 643 men, of 655 crew and 12 passengers, who were drowned or died of exposure, and his body was never found. The wreck is listed under the Protection of Military Remains Act and a crenellated tower stands on Marwick Head in memory of Kitchener.

·Further on, at Mainland's north-west edge, is Brough Head and Brough of Birsay, a tidal island with the remains of a Viking settlement that was built on the site of an earlier, Pictish village. A Pictish enclosure round a Norse church has yielded an eighth century stone slab showing symbols and three figures in pro-

cession, dressed in long robes and carrying spears, swords and shields. Brough of Birsay may be visited (and you may inspect a replica of the slab) but time your visit well to coincide with its causeway being uncovered by the retreating tide.

Overlooking Brough of Birsay may be found the remains of Earl Robert Stew-

ABOVE Cloud formation above a beach on Stronsay, Orkney

art's Palace. Rebuilt between 1569 and 1579, it stands as a monument to the illegitimate son of James V's royal pretensions and his oppression of the Orcadians. A two-storey palace built around a central courtyard and well, it has large stone towers at three of its four corners, and was where the ancient earls of Orkney resided before moving to Kirkwall.

Turning southwards on Mainland's east coast, you will come across Broch of Gurness, otherwise known as Aikerness Broch. In Orkney, brochs were usually surrounded by sizeable villages, and this is the case here. Gurness is a well-preserved broch, and its village was begun between 500 and 2000BC. An area 45 metres in diameter was defined by deep ditches and ramparts, an entrance causeway was added on the east side and a circular broch tower was built in the west half. Around the tower was a settlement of stone houses with yards and sheds. The broch was abandoned and the ditches filled in some time after 100AD, but the site continued to be used as a farmstead until around the eighth century. As a final act, in the ninth century a Viking woman and her grave goods were buried at Gurness.

Take a little diversion from the coast, six kilometres south-west of Gurness

Broch, to discover Orkney's last surviving click mill – a horizontal water mill once common throughout Orkney and Shetland as well as Lewis – at Dounby.

In the Bay of Firth, north of Kirkwall, is the island of Damsay, which is mentioned in the *Orkneyinga Sagas*. It appears that when Erlend and Sweyn were at war with the earls Rognvald and Harald, Erlend overdid the celebrations at Christmas on Damsay and fell into a drunken sleep on his ship. It was a fatal mistake, for he and his men were surprised and killed by the enemy.

Graemsay, an inhabited island that boasts two lighthouses, Flotta (site of a major oil terminal) and the smaller isles of Cava, Fara and Switha lie between Mainland and Hoy, the second largest island in Orkney. Of all the islands in the archipelago, this is the wildest and wettest, gathering an average annual rainfall of 1500 millimetres.

Hoy (area: 14,000 hectares; population: more than 400) is also the highest island of Orkney, having Ward Hill, at 479 metres, at its centre. Local legend states that there used to be a huge carbuncle on the north side of Ward Hill that glowed red in the dark but dimmed and disappeared whenever it was approached. The island also has some of the highest sea cliffs in the UK, towering to 350 metres at St John's Head on the north-west coast and the unforgettable sight of the 137 metre sea stack the Old Man of Hoy to the south.

Greeting travellers on the ferry from Scrabster, the Old Man appears from some angles to have a human form. Formed of red sandstone, it is no more than a few hundred years old, having been separated from the cliffs by the relentless action of the waves in the 18th century. It's a popular challenge for climbers who don't mind braving the high winds, having first been conquered as recently as 1966, but the sad news is that the Old Man of Hoy may soon be no more: experts seem quite confident in predicting its collapse. The question is when.

To the east of St John's Head, in the Rackwick Valley, is the Dwarfie Stane, a megalithic chambered tomb – the only one in Orkney that is cut from, rather than built from, stones. It is possibly Britain's only example of a Neolithic rock-cut tomb, more usually found in the Mediterranean region. Consisting of a passage and two chambers, the tomb gets its name

from the legend that a dwarf called Trollid lived in it, but other sources claim it was the abode of giants.

The dwarf connections continue in the Dwarfie Hamars, under which the tomb lies: the cliff face is said to be named after the dwarfs who forged the hammer of the Norse god Thor. And the nearby Trowie Glen's name comes from the Old Norse word troll – an ugly cave-dwelling creature depicted as either a dwarf or a giant.

There is more fascinating stuff to be discovered on Hoy. In the far north you may find the Kame of Hoy, the second highest peak on the island at 433 metres and the neighbour of the Valley of the Seven Echoes. Here a shout from the middle of the valley will be returned sevenfold. And Rackwick on the west coast is described by Hamish Haswell-Smith as Orkney's most isolated spot. The author memorably tells of the former days of this fishing village, when its men were known as fine dancers who would walk six kilometres over the hills to Hoy village, dance the night away and then walk home again, no doubt to take to their boats for their work as fishermen.

The northern part of Hoy is an RSPB reserve noted for its great skuas and red-throated divers. In the south-east is the village of Lyness, the main base of the British

ABOVE Pier on Papa Westray, Orkney

Scapa Flow fleet in both world wars. To the south of the village, guarding the natural harbour of Longhope, are two Martello Towers, built to defend the island during the Napoleonic Wars but never used.

Hoy's extreme south is connected by a causeway to South Walls; the two islands are regarded as one entity by the UK Census. South Walls has a healthy population and, naturally, its fair share of remains of the naval occupation of the area during World War II.

Shapinsay, an island of nearly 3,000 hectares and a population of over 300, lies to the north of Mainland. It's delightful to learn that its name comes from the Old Norse for 'helpful island', perhaps because of its good harbour.

The village of Balfour in the south-west, the destination for ferries from Kirkwall, is dominated by the castle that bears its name and was built in 1847 on the site of an older structure. It's now run as a hotel – 'the world's most northerly island castle available for exclusive use' according to its marketing material. Quholm, in the island's north-east, was home to the parents of William Washington Irving, author of the story of Rip Van Winkle and remembered as the father of American literature.

To the north-east of Shapinsay is Stronsay, which measures up at 3,275 hectares and has a population of around 350. Arriving here on a ferry from Kirkwall, you will find the settlement of Whitehall, which nowadays has a hotel, a pub, shops and a heritage centre but was once a boom town. Whitehall's history mirrors the rise and fall of the herring industry, for it was once the most active port in Orkney catering to that trade. There were at one time around 300 boats in Papa Sound, in the north-east, 15 curing stations, around 1,500 fishwives and 40 pubs. The village's one-time prosperity can be seen from the large houses that dominate it.

Man has inhabited Stronsay for a long, long time. Two flint arrowheads found on a farm in 2007 are thought to date from the late Palaolithic or early Meso-lithic periods, which would mean they are between 10,000 and 12,000 years old. That being the case – and it is yet to be confirmed – they could be the oldest human artefacts ever found in Scotland.

As ever in Orkney, wonderful legends are to be found on this low-lying island. One concerns the Mermaid's Chair, a rock seat on the beach that runs around Mill Bay in the east. It's recounted that Scota Bess was a storm witch who would sit here dispensing evil spells, to the despair of the local people. Having beaten the witch to death they buried her, but in the morning her body was found lying beside the grave – and this happened several times. Eventually the villagers threw the corpse into Meikle Water and that was the end of that. But any girl who sits in the Mermaid's Chair will be able to predict the future; or so it's said.

Stronsay is also home to the memorable Vat of Kirbister, which has been called the most spectacular rock arch in Orkney. Situated on the south-east coast, this is where the roof of a large, almost circular cave has collapsed, leaving an inlet accessible via the original cave mouth and under the arch.

Much closer to the northern coast of Mainland is Rousay, an island that has been described as the Egypt of the North because of its archaeological importance and diversity. Some authorities say that Rousay is perhaps the most interesting island in all of Orkney, and point to its advantage in that some of the best sites are quite near the ferry pier on the south coast.

Upon leaving the ferry across the Eynhallow Sound from Tingwall, turn west and you are soon in the vicinity of three extraordinary burial cairns: Taversoe Tuick, Blackhammer and Knowe of Yarso. But that's not all. On Rousay you can find evidence from every era in the history of Orkney. Findings include the remains of a Neolithic settlement at Rinyo; Bronze Age burnt mounds (heaps of shattered stones and charcoal, usually with an adjacent hearth and trough); the highest density of Iron Age crannogs and brochs in Scotland; Viking boat burials; the remains of a medieval church; and a

19th century stately home at Trumland in the south. Such is the weight of archaeological sites – more than 100 have been identified – that only a small number have been excavated.

One site that has been well researched is halfway up the west coast of Rousay. Midhowe Broch, dating from the Iron Age, is part of a settlement that has been partly lost to coastal erosion. Its tower, formed by walls 4.5 metres thick, measures nine metres across and is full of stone partitions. On the floor is a spring-fed water tank and a hearth with sockets that may once have held a roasting spit.

Nearby is Midhowe Chambered Cairn, which predates that of Maeshowe on Mainland. Twelve burial chambers flank a passageway that is nearly 24 metres in length. Transverse stones reach a height of two metres and the walls still rise to 2.5 metres. The cairn appears to have been deliberately filled with debris after a few hundred years of use, beginning early in the third millennium BC. It was originally protected by an oval barrow 33 metres long and 13 metres wide and supported by three concentric stone casing walls. The remains of at least 25 people were discovered in Midhowe, as well as bones from many animals.

Rousay, the hilliest Orkney island after

Hoy, is also the fifth largest at nearly 5,000 hectares. Around 200 people live here, most of them employed in farming and fishing. A single road circles the island, and most of the arable land lies in the few hundred metres between it and the coast.

Egilsay (2011 population: 26), lying to the east of Rousay, is much smaller at 650 hectares. Shaped like a spearhead, its most remarkable feature is Saint Magnus Church, which has a 12th century round tower in the Irish style that is nowadays the only one of its kind in Orkney. It is not the place where Saint Magnus kept vigil before his death, but the site of the murder is quite near and is marked by a stone cenotaph.

Even smaller than Egilsay but supporting a similar-sized population is Wyre, which lies off Rousay's south coast. This is the location of what is perhaps the earliest stone castle to have survived in Scotland: Cubbie Roo's Castle. Named after Kolbein Hruga (of whom more later) and dating from around 1150, it is to be found in the centre of the island and takes the form of a stone keep about 7.5 metres square surrounded by a stone-faced ditch. It is recorded in one of the Norse sagas that the killers of Earl John, the last Norse Earl of Orkney, fled from Thurso to Wyre and took refuge in the castle in 1231. Such

was the strength of the castle that their besiegers were forced to arrange a truce before the matter could be resolved.

Wyre is also notable for its roofless 12th century St Mary's Chapel, whose architecture displays Romanesque traits – evidence that the Vikings absorbed influences wherever they travelled, raided and traded.

The island folk used to attribute the character of a lumbering giant to Kolbein Hruga, aka Cubbie Roo. He was so enormous that he could walk from island to island but was frustrated when he tried to build bridges and causeways because the stones kept breaking his kishie (straw basket used for carrying peat). And that's why there are so many skerries and rocks lying scattered around the islands.

The island of Eday is to the east and north of Egilsay. This is a place of 2,745 hectares and a population of 160 whose name means 'isthmus island', referring to the 500 metre wide neck of land at its centre, separating the Sands of Doomy and Bay of London. That is the site of an airstrip, but the island can also be reached by ferry from Mainland. Eday's inhabitants are scattered along farms on the coasts and there is nowhere with the status of village.

This is another island with more than its fair share of prehistoric remains, including a number of chambered cairns. The one at Vinquoy, overlooking the Calf Sound on the north-east coast, is 17 metres in diameter and 2.5 metres high. One of the tallest monoliths in Orkney can be found in the Stone of Setter standing stone, which resembles a giant hand and reaches five metres upwards. It is located near Mill Loch in the north of the island.

Eday has rich deposits of peat, which were much in demand among Orcadians in the 18th and 19th centuries, and its slate was another valuable export. The growth of coal as a fuel meant the island's prosperity was not to last.

Beyond Faray to Eday's north-west lies Westray, often referred to as the Queen of the North Isles. This is an island of 4,700 hectares and nearly 600 residents whose prosperity relies on cattle farming, fishing and a combination of the two: fish farming. It's also an island that is rich in history.

It's believed that Westray and its little neighbour, Papa Westray were joined at the time of its earliest known settlements, in about 3500BC. Nowadays they are linked by the world's shortest scheduled flight. Links of Noltland on the north coast contains the remains of both a Neolithic village and later Bronze Age houses. Here it was that the Westray Wife – a loz-enge-shaped figurine believed to be Scotland's earliest representation of a human face – was found in 2009. The Wife, carved from sandstone, has dots for eyes, heavy brows, an oblong nose and patterns on the body that may represent clothing. She is thought to have been created between 2500 and 3000BC. Incredibly, two further figurines were found in 2010 and 2012, and the extent of Links of Noltland is thought to exceed that of Skara Brae.

Near the village of Pierowall, tucked away on the east coast, is Noltland Castle, which dates mainly from the later 16th century and is described by the authority on Scottish islands Hamish Haswell-Smith as mysterious. Why? Because it is unclear why such a mammoth structure was ever built at that location. At Pierowall itself can be found a dry-stone Atlantic roundhouse dating to the Iron Age, and a heritage centre does a good job of telling the island's history.

Papa Westray, known as Papay to Orcadians, lies to the north of Westray and is home to nearly 100 people. On the west coast of the 'priest island' is located the Neolithic farmstead Knap of Howar. Occupied from 3700 to 2800BC, this is perhaps the oldest preserved stone house in northern Europe. The farmstead consists of two rounded but rectangular thick-

RIGHT The Old Beacon
lighthouse on North
Ronaldsay, Orkney

walled buildings with low doorways facing the sea. The larger, older building is linked by a passageway to the other building, which was perhaps a workshop or perhaps a second house.

On the other side of the island is the ruined Chapel of Saint Tredwell, dedicated to a remarkable eighth century girl. The Pictish king Nechtan is said to have told Tredwell, or Triduana, that he intended to rape her, whereupon she plucked out her own eyes and handed them to him, putting him off the idea somewhat. The chapel that bears her name became a place of pilgrimage for those with eye complaints.

Venturing eastwards will bring the island of Sanday ('island of sand') into view. Here you have a population of nearly 500 inhabiting an island of 5,000 hectares – the third largest in Orkney. It's believed that Sanday was mostly underwater at some points in prehistory, and the evidence suggests that there were several islands hereabouts that joined up when the sea level fell.

As elsewhere in Orkney, the island is pinpricked with important ancient monuments. One is the Quoyness chambered cairn on the south-east coast, in which the bones of 10 adults and five children were discovered in the 1860s. Each Stone Age burial site like this was said to have its own resident hogboon, a bad-tempered being who would cause trouble for any human who disturbed him.

In 1991 a Viking ship burial was found north-east of Scar on the northern peninsula of Burness. Dated to between 875 and 950AD, the burial contained the remains of a man, an elderly woman and a child, with many grave goods. The wood of the 6.5 metre boat in which they had been buried – inside a stone-lined enclosure – had rotted away but the site is still of major importance.

Most northerly of the islands of Orkney is North Ronaldsay, which has a population of around 70 for its 700 hectares. Nowhere on the island is higher than 20 metres above sea level and it's exposed to the elements, but it is widely cultivated and speckled with cottages. Flights and a weekly ferry link North Ronaldsay with Kirkwall.

This island is home to a flock of small, primitive, goat-like sheep, which exist on a diet of seaweed except when they are lambing. Their presence necessitated the building of the two-metre Sheep Dyke, which encircles the entire island and ensures that the sheep stay on the seashore, where they can do no damage to agricultural produce.

In 1993 a great storm destroyed more than three of the dyke's 20 kilometres and the sheep were left free to roam the interior, before hasty repairs were effected with the help of the Royal Navy.

East of Loch Gretchen, in the southwest of the island (where you might want to avail yourself of a hide that gives an excellent view of the birdlife) is the curious four-metre Stan Stane standing stone, pierced by a hole in its upper part. In former times this was the scene of much celebration on New Year's Eve, when the islanders would dance around the stone. Sadly, it seems that the meaning of this ritual has been lost with the passing of time.

North Ronaldsay's waters are notoriously treacherous and its lighthouse, built in 1854 to replace an earlier structure whose lights were often mistaken for the masthead of a ship, is a welcome sight for seafarers. Sited at Dennis Head in the north-east, this is the tallest land-based lighthouse in the British Isles at 33 metres, yet it could not help the three German ships that ran aground, one after another, one day in March 1926.

There are still more islands to be discovered north of North Ronaldsay. Eighty kilometres to the north-east lie the captivating isles of Shetland.

Shetland

You will have to go a long way to find an island chain as engagingly distinctive as Shetland. Come to that, you will have to go a long way to find Shetland.

This archipelago of more than 100 islands, 15 of them inhabited, lies 80 kilometres north-east of Orkney if you don't count Fair Isle, which is regarded as part of Shetland for administrative purposes but sits nearly 40 kilometres from the chain's biggest island of Mainland. London is nearly 1,000 kilometres away. Between Fair Isle in the south and Out Stack in the north, Shetland stretches for 145 kilometres. The numerous islands of Shetland form a barrier between the North Atlantic to the west and the North Sea to the east.

And there's more than a geographical gap between Shetland and the rest of the UK. You will find here a beguiling blend of Scottish and Scandinavian culture, the result of the islands' status as part of the Norse earldom that was based in Orkney until their annexation to Scotland in 1471. Even now, studies of the islanders' genetic make-up show that Shetlanders are just under half Scandinavian in origin, and just about every place name can be traced back to the Vikings. The Scots dialect spoken in the islands, Shetlandic, contains many Old Norse words, and many houses are built in a Scandinavian style. And Shetlanders celebrate their Norse heritage in style with festivities such as Up Helly Aa annual fire festivals in which Viking galleys are burned.

The 22,500 people of Shetland nowadays contribute to an economy that re-

lies on agriculture and fishing but has received a massive boost from the oil industry, which is worth £100 million a year to the islands. In addition, tourists flock to the islands to take in their spectacular coastlines, their rich wildlife and their intriguing abundance of archaeological sites, as well as their ever-popular knitted goods. Talking of the latter, where better to start a tour of Shetland than in Fair Isle.

Lying roughly midway between North Ronaldsay in Orkney and Sumburgh Head on the Mainland of Shetland, Fair Isle is the UK's most remote inhabited island. It's a place of 770 hectares and a sparse population of around 70, most of whom live in crofts in the southern part of the island. The north consists of rocky moorland while Fair Isle's west coast boasts dramatic cliffs up to 200 metres high. The island's highest point is at Ward Hill in the northwest, which reaches 217 metres.

Birdwatchers find their own kind of heaven on this island, for it is home to the Fair Isle Bird Observatory, where research on migration and seabird breeding colonies has been carried out for more than 50 years. The autumn and spring migration periods attract visitors hoping to see rarities such as the lanceolated warbler and Pallas's grasshopper warbler, for example, and at other times the cliffs resound to the sound of fulmars, razorbills, puffins, guillemots, skuas and kittiwakes among many other species. Catered accommodation is available at the observatory's lodge.

Fair Isle has a worldwide reputation for its knitting, and it's due to the islanders who discovered long ago that fine yarns stranded into a double layer make for clothes that are durable, warm and lightweight. For centuries, the women of the island knitted the goods for trade with the occupants of passing ships. Nowadays the world's only genuine Fair Isle sweaters are produced by a small co-operative on hand-frame machines, although there are many imitators of lesser quality throughout the world attempting the colourful knitting with horizontal bands of geometric patterns.

The island is also known for the number of ships that have sunk on its dangerous coast over the centuries. There are around 100 known wrecks scattered around Fair Isle, but one of the best known is that of *El Gran Grifon*, a ship of the Spanish Armada of 1588. Three hundred soldiers and sailors were stranded on

LEFT Purple toadflax on Fair Isle, Shetland

RIGHT Inside Mousa
Broch, Mousa, Shetland

Fair Isle after their vessel foundered in the cove of Stroms Heelor in the south-east.

Fair Isle can be reached by ferry or plane from Mainland, Shetland's biggest island by far at nearly 100,000 hectares and the fifth largest in the British Isles. Nearly 19,000 people have their homes on an island that can be divided roughly into four main parts: the long southern peninsula that dangles 40 kilometres south of the capital Lerwick (a burgh of 7,500 inhabitants); a central part composed mainly of farmland and woodland; the west, which offers wonderful beaches and hill and coastal walks; and the wild moorland of the north including the Northmavine peninsula with its cliff landscapes.

The South Mainland has some of Shetland's most productive farmland, red sandstone rocks, secluded coves, shell sand beaches and marvellous views from Scousburgh Hill and Fitful Head in the extreme south-west. Outlying islands connected by bridges to Mainland include East and West Burra, the latter of which contains the busy fishing port of Hamna Voe.

If you travel south from Lerwick on the east, you'll pass Quarff and go through Cunningsburgh and then perceive the small island of Mousa lying off the coast.

This is the location of Mousa Broch, the best preserved Iron Age fortification in the British Isles and probably the world. A 2,000-year-old round tower, 15 metres in diameter, rises 13 metres to guard Mousa Sound. Virtually intact, its internal diameter is a mere six metres, smaller than most other brochs in Scotland, but that doesn't stop visitors climbing the stairs and gaining a rewarding view.

Mousa fell out of use between 200 and 500AD, although it was reoccupied in 1153 when an eloping couple, Margaret (mother of Earl Harald) and Erlend found it suited their purpose. Earl Harald, not impressed by his mother's behaviour, laid siege to the broch but found it 'an unhandy place to get at'. All turned out well with the newly married couple ferried to Norway for their honeymoon by none other than Harald.

South of Mousa on the Mainland is the Shetland Crofthouse Museum, a thatched homestead that has been restored to how it would have looked 100 years ago. Carry on towards Sumburgh Head and you will come to the Iron Age village of Old Scatness, where many of the buildings are still standing at or near roof height and some are even still decorated with yellow clay. And then, less than a mile on from

Old Scatness, is Jarlshof, which has been described as one of the most remarkable archaeological sites ever excavated in the British Isles.

Exposed by storms at the end of the 19th century, the settlement tells the story of 4,000 years of human history with a series of stone structures: late Neolithic houses, a Bronze Age village, an Iron Age broch and wheelhouses, a Norse long-house, a medieval farmstead and a 16th century laird's house. Given its name by Sir Walter Scott in his novel *The Pirate* (he thought it sounded more romantic than Sumburgh), Jarlshof means 'earl's house', but that really is just a small part of the story.

Sumburgh Head is topped by Shet-land's first lighthouse and has the UK's most accessible colony of puffins – or tammie nories as the Shetlanders call them. There are more birds to be seen on the Loch of Spiggie after you round the southern tip and head north, and then you will spy St Ninian's Isle, linked to Mainland by a tombolo beach. The isle became famous when a young boy helping at an archaeological dig at the tiny Celtic chapel found a hoard of silver bowls and ornaments, believed to date from around 800AD. Replicas are on dis-

LEFT Hay's Dock in Lerwick, Shetland

play at the Shetland Museum in Lerwick.

The west coast fishing port of Scalloway, Shetland's capital until the 18th century, is shielded from the Atlantic weather by the isles of Trondra and Burra. Overlooking the harbour is Scalloway Castle, built by forced labour for Earl Patrick Stewart in 1600. Beneath its banqueting hall is a dungeon where witches of the 17th century awaited the execution of their death sentences on nearby Gallows Hill.

Lerwick ('mud creek') was founded as an unofficial marketplace to serve Dutch herring fleets in the 17th century, and its illegal status brought punishment in the form of demolition on the orders of the Scalloway Court in 1615 and 1625. Further disasters followed when the Dutch and the French set fire to the town in 1673 and 1702 respectively. Despite these setbacks, Lerwick is now a busy seaport with all the facilities visitors might want. Worth a visit are the Town Hall, which contains a Victorian interpretation of a Viking drinking hall, and the Shetland Museum.

On the last Tuesday of every January, Lerwick is the scene of the biggest of Shetland's Up Helly Aa fire festivals, which celebrate of the end of the Yule season. On the evening of Up Helly Aa Day, more than 800 disguised men, or guizers,

process through the streets armed with blazing torches. Their leader, the Guizer Jarl, stands at the helm of a replica Viking longship, which is dragged through the streets through crowds of spectators before being set on fire by torches hurled by the guizers. Then the partying can start, and carry on all night. Thankfully, the following day is a public holiday.

The island of Bressay, lying opposite Lerwick, has the even smaller isle of Noss off its east coast. On Bressay (area: 2,800 hectares; 2011 population: 368) can be found an old kirkyard lying partly over a ruined broch. This is the site of the discovery of the Bressay Stone, which appears to be a memorial to the daughter of a Pictish chieftain, Naddod, and is inscribed with Ogham script, which has never been fully deciphered. There is a replica on the site.

The cliffs of Noss offer one of the most spectacular wildlife sights anywhere in the world. At the peak of the breeding season the deafening chorus of 150,000 birds and chicks fills the air, as does the smell of the guano that stains the cliffs white. It's not Britain's biggest seabird colony but Noss is perhaps the most accessible, combining huge numbers of birds with a wide variety of species and spectacular scenery.

To the west of Lerwick is Tingwall Loch and at its north end is the Lawting Holm, a promontory that was the seat of the Shetland parliament in Norse times; the word Tingwall comes from the same root as Tynwald, the Isle of Man's parliament.

The west of Mainland offers beautiful beaches, exhilarating walks on hills and at the coast, all kinds of wildlife and interesting historical and archaeological sites. The coastline varies from cliffs to long sea lochs, or voes, that reach far inland. This area is home to some of Shetland's keenest gardeners and visitors speak highly of the garden at Burrastow House near the village of Walls in the west, among others.

Lying off the north-west of west Mainland is Papa Stour ('big island of the priests'), an island formed from volcanic lava and ash and then carved by the sea to form some of the most spectacular sea caves in Britain. Perhaps the finest of them all is Kirstan Hol, on the south-west of the island. At the head of a narrow creek, between vertical 30 metre rock faces, stands a rock stack beside a 27 metre wide arch that forms the cave's entrance. The cave continues for about 70 metres before ending at a beach.

Papa Stour is a low-lying, fertile island of 800-odd hectares that is home to about

LEFT The island of Noss seen from Bressay, Shetland

20 people, most of whom are engaged in crofting. Local people tell the story of a strange ship that sailed into Housa Voe on the east of the island. The crew seemed to be ready to attack the settlement but they were repelled by the work of the local witch, Minna Baaba, who called up a storm to drive the ship far out to sea.

Off the eastern coast of the north of Mainland lies Whalsay (Whale Island), an island of nearly 2,000 hectares and more than 1,000 residents. Here, after leaving the ferry from Laxo on Mainland, you will find the UK's most northerly golf course as well as the centre of Shetland's fishing industry. Watch out during the ferry crossing for porpoises, dolphins, minke whales and orcas.

The harbour at Symbister is crowded with vessels owned and crewed by local families, from small creel boats to massive ocean-going trawlers. The Whalsay Heritage Centre, also in Symbister, mounts exhibitions throughout the year. The museum in the Pier House tells how ships from Hamburg, Bremen and Lubeck sailed to Shetland to bring seeds, cloth, iron tools, salt, spirits, luxury goods and currency. Some of those merchants are buried in the islands.

Naturally, the folklore of Whalsay is rich. It tells of a water demon known as the njuggle that inhabits Nuckro Water and usually appears as a friendly horse. Once its gullible victim is mounted on its back, the njuggle carries him or her out into the water and death by drowning.

This island inspired some of the best work created by Hugh MacDiarmid, a 20th century poet who dubbed Whalsay 'the bonnie isle' and lived here during the 1930s. He was regarded as something of an oddity by the islanders, who witnessed his frequent visits to the post office to conduct a heated correspondence with other writers.

Further out to the east lie the Out Skerries, an island group that forms the easternmost point of Scotland. The main islands are Housay, Bruray (both inhabited) and Grunay. More than 70 people live on these 400 hectares of rock and pasture. During the spring and autumn migrations Skerries, as local people call them, can rival Fair Isle for sightings of rare birds; this is the first landfall after flocks leave Norway.

Back on Mainland and north of Lerwick, the Nesting Loop side road winds through a landscape of sheltered inlets, scattered crofts and headlands. The Catfirth and Quoys Burns have relics of the woodland that once covered Shetland. Passing the Loch of Benston will bring you to the promontory of Gletness, one of this part of the world's most beautiful corners and home to a stud of Shetland ponies.

North of Nesting lies Lunnasting, in which sits Vidlin, an ancient settlement with an Iron Age broch lying under the Methodist kirk. The landscape of Lunnasting is formed from schist and gneiss rocks, formed over 500 million years ago and carved by ice into whale-backed hills and long inlets. The road north from Vidlin leads to Lunna, where there is a tiny church dating from 1753, the oldest in continuous use in Shetland. Not far away are the mysterious Stanes of Stofast – a 2,000 tonne 'glacial erratic' boulder, sledged from Norway on the ice and split in two by frost. This is a heavily glaciated landscape with eerily shaped rocks associated with the trows (trolls) of Shetland folklore.

Delting, north-west of Lunnasting, has seen many changes since the discovery of oil off Shetland. Hundreds of new homes needed to accommodate the workforce were built in Voe, Brae, Firth and Mossbank.

The old village of Voe at the head of Olna Firth has a distinctly Norwegian character. Beyond Busta is the ruggedly beautiful island of Muckle Roe, linked to the mainland by a bridge. Here contraband from Faroe was once landed in the Hams (havens). In a former quarry beside the road to Scotland's largest sea loch, Sullom Voe, geologists have identified rocks altered by heat and pressure 400 million years ago when, as the ancient Iapetus Ocean closed, the European and North American tectonic plates collided.

The Sullom Voe oil terminal, the largest export terminal of its kind in Europe, handles up to 40 million tonnes of oil and gas a year but strict environmental controls have minimised its impact on the area and the voe is still home to a wide range of wildlife.

In the extreme north-west of Mainland, the parish of Northmavine has some of the finest views and best hill and coastal walking in Shetland. In between the rugged coastline and hills are dozens of small crofting settlements, making this one of the islands' prettiest places.

Almost but not quite a separate island, Northmavine is joined to the rest of the Shetland Mainland at Mavis Grind. From here you enter a landscape dominated by the archipelago's highest peak, Ronas Hill (450 metres), at the top of which is a chambered burial cairn. The view from

SHETLAND

Sunrise
in Shetland

RIGHT Passing place
on Unst, Shetland

Ronas Hill can, on a clear day, show all of Shetland and, if you are very lucky, even Fair Isle. To the north lie ice-carved low hills and dozens of freshwater lochs. To the north-east are the jagged rocks of the Ramna Stacks, with background silhouettes of the Gloup Holm in North Yell and the Muckle Flugga rocks north of Unst.

Before we leave Mainland, we should cast our eyes far, far to the west to pick out the lonely island of Foula, 20 kilometres west of Walls. In 2011 this 1,200-hectare island was inhabited by 38 people living in the settlements of Hametown and Ham, where they observe the Julian calendar unlike the rest of Britain, which abandoned it for the Gregorian calendar a little matter of 260 years ago. This place is so isolated that 90 per cent of the population died when smallpox hit the island in 1720 – unlike the rest of northern Europe they had not developed some immunity to the virus. It takes the thrice-weekly ferry from Walls more than two hours to reach Ham Voe on Foula's east coast. Not for nothing was the 1937 movie *The Edge of the World* filmed here.

On the west side can be found Shetland's biggest and most spectacular cliffs, reaching as high as 365 metres. Five peaks – Da Noup, Hamnafield, Da Kame, Soberlie and Da Sneug – dominate the island, with Da Sneug rising to 418 metres of loveliness. Three kilometres east of the island lies the hidden reef of Hoevdi Grund, or the Shaalds o' Foula, which comes to within a few feet of the sea's surface and presents a major threat to shipping.

Some residents nowadays earn their living from ornithological tourism, such is the interest in what the Norsemen called Bird Island. Foula provides a research station for zoologists from Glasgow University who study the world's largest colony of great skuas – known as bonxies to the islanders – and much other birdlife besides.

The sizeable island of Yell (the name might mean 'barren', belying the rich peat deposits) lies north-east of Mainland. It's an island of 21,000 hectares and nearly 1,000 inhabitants that lays claim to the title of otter capital of Britain. A car ferry service operates from Toft on Mainland to Ulsta on Yell.

This is a place of bleak aspect where the residents live mostly on the coasts. One writer noted in the 16th century that

Yell was 'so uncouth a place that no creature can live therein, except such as are born there', but that does the place an injustice. Yell has been inhabited since the Neolithic age and has a dozen broch sites dating from before the Norsemen arrived.

The main settlement is that of Burravoe in the south-east. Here you will find the Old Haa of Brough, built for a merchant in 1672 and nowadays home to a museum and heritage centre dedicated to the history and folklore of the island. One permanent exhibit is a propeller from an RAF Catalina flying boat that crashed on the hill above Burravoe in 1942, killing seven of her 10 passengers. At the northern end of Yell, at Gloup, is a memorial to 58 fishermen who drowned when a storm swept unexpectedly down from Iceland in 1881.

The island of Fetlar, lying off Yell's east coast, sounds like a good place to live – its name comes from the Old Norse for fat or prosperous land. This is the fourth largest island of Shetland at a little over 4,000 hectares and supports a population of some 60 inhabitants. Its fertile soil was a big attraction to prospective settlers, and local tradition has it that the Wick of Gruting in the island's north-east provided the first landfall in Shetland for Norsemen, although this is disputed by Haroldswick in Unst.

Most visitors to Fetlar are puzzled by the obvious presence of a large wall that divides the island in two, running from north to south. Originally a metre wide, Funzie Girt, or the Finnigirt Dyke as it's also known, now begins in the north by the cliffs of Muckle Funzigord Geo, crosses an RSPB reserve to the west of Vord Hill then vanishes near Whilsa Pund. It reappears at the southern shore of Skutes Water but is lost again as it skirts the southern settlement of Houbie to reach the south coast at a point unknown. Its original length was thus around four kilometres. Despite centuries of theories about territorial disputes and suchlike, no one knows when or why it was built. You are free to inspect what remains of Funzie Girt and arrive at your own hypothesis.

Fetlar holds further mysteries in the form of three enigmatic stone circles, each about 13.5 metres in diameter, standing between Vord Hill and Skutes Water. They are set in a triangular pattern so that they almost touch each other. And not far away is a circle of stones ringing an internal, concentric earth bank and two central stones that is known by the name of Haltadans ('limping dance'). Experts cannot explain the significance of these structures, but folklore can come to the rescue. It's an obvious explanation: a local fiddler and his wife were dancing in the moonlight one night with a number of trolls. Such was their preoccupation with their enjoyment that they failed to anticipate the dawn, and they were all instantly turned to stone by the sun's rays.

If you want to visit the most northerly of Scotland's inhabited islands, you will make your way to Unst by ferry from Yell. And here you will find Shetland in miniature, crammed into an island of 12,000 hectares, 20 kilometres long by eight wide: spectacular cliffs, rugged sea stacks, rocky shores, golden beaches, freshwater lochs scattered among the peat bogs and farmlands and even something of a novelty, a sub-Arctic stony desert.

The main village on Unst is Baltasound, located in a sheltered east coast bay called, unsurprisingly, Balta Sound. The tiny isle of Balta lies at the bay's mouth. Once the second largest herring port in Shetland after Lerwick, the village now boasts a brewery and an airport. Further north, in Haroldswick, you may spend some time at the Boat Haven, which harbours boats of various types that have been in use hereabouts for the past 150 years. Haroldswick is also the location of the northernmost post office in the UK, and you may have your postcards franked to that effect here.

Across the Burra Firth from Saxa Vord (284 metres), the highest peak in Unst, the peninsula of Hermaness is a wilderness that seems to have been untouched by human feet, although it's an area worth visiting for its wildlife and its tales of the giants Herman and his rival Saxi.

So we come to the inevitable list of 'the most northerly' places. Haroldswick also claims the northernmost church in the British Isles. The tiny settlement of Skaw is the last inhabited place in the UK. The Muckle Flugga lighthouse, opened in 1858 and perched on a tiny island of the same name, is the most northerly of all of Scotland's lighthouses. Six hundred metres north of Muckle Flugga sits the rocky outcrop of Out Stack, and then there's nothing, if you're heading directly north, until you hit the North Pole. It's said that Lady Franklin, waiting for the return of her explorer husband Sir John in 1849, landed on Out Stack and prayed. Her prayers were in vain.

Chapter 7

Firth of Forth

Unlike the Atlantic-facing west, the east coast of Scotland is not studded with little pieces of heaven in the form of islands. Nor are there any centres of human population here; the islands that do exist are more likely to be inhabited by vast colonies of seabirds. Some 'islands' are no more than particularly chunky rocks. The few of any size to be found in this part of the world are grouped in the Firth of Forth where the river Forth becomes one with the North Sea, between Fife to the north and Lothian to the south.

The furthest east of these is the Isle of May, a sill of volcanic rock to be found south of the East Neuk of Fife. May measures a mere 45 hectares, being 1.8 kilometres long and less than half a kilo-metre wide, and no one lives here now, but humans have been coming here for at least 4,000 years. Bronze Age flint arrowheads and stone axes have been found to prove it.

An Irish missionary established a shrine or small church on the island before meeting his death at the hands of Vikings in 669AD. But in 1145 St Adrian's Priory was established and was home to up to 13 monks at a time. The ruined manor house you can now see on the Isle of May was built on the foundations of the priory and church. In 1636, Alexander Cunningham built Scotland's first lighthouse on the island to guide shipping in one of Scotland's busiest waterways. Fired by coal, the Beacon claimed victims of carbon monoxide poisoning in 1791 and was replaced in

1816 by Robert Stevenson's Main Light.

The way to get to the island is by a 45-minute ferry journey from Anstruther or Crail, and visitors are assured of a noisy welcome, especially in nesting season. The west cliffs are notable for their rock stacks, arches and caves and, of course, the birds, of which there are many. A bird observatory was opened here as early as 1934.

To the south-west of the Isle of May, about two kilometres offshore and facing the ruins of Tantallon Castle on the mainland, the Bass Rock is the home of a colony of gannets up to 150,000 strong. That's why the gannet's scientific name is Sula Bassana, and why Sir David Attenborough called the Bass 'one of the 12 wildlife wonders of the world'.

The remains of one of many volcanoes that have played an important role in the geology of this part of Scotland, this imposing rock was formed 320 million years ago. It has been called the Ailsa Craig of the east although it's much smaller than its western relative. A mere three hectares in area, it rises to 107 metres, and a gentler slope to the south forms a lower promontory where you may see the ruins of a castle dating back to at least 1405.

LEFT Inchcolm Abbey, Inchcolm, Firth of Forth

The first inhabitant was Saint Baldred, who was sent by Saint Mungo to spread Christianity to the Lothians in the sixth century. He founded a monastery at Tyninghame and later lived as a hermit on the Bass. About halfway up the Rock are the ruins of a chapel said to mark the location of the saint's cell.

For centuries in the possession of the Lauder family, the Bass is now uninhabited, but its lighthouse still has an important function. It was built in 1902 by David Stevenson, who demolished parts of the castle for the stone.

Of the other islands in the firth, Inchkeith, lying roughly between Leith and Kinghorn, is of particular interest. Its last inhabitants departed the 23 hectare island in 1986, leaving behind a rich history. Inchkeith ('wooded island') has in its time been the seat of Pictish kings, a base for early Christian evangelists, an isolation colony for sufferers from syphilis and the plague, a fortress, the scene of a bloody battle and the site of heavy gun emplacements during the two world wars.

What's more, in 1493 Inchkeith was the site of a weird experiment in which King James IV directed that a woman who could not speak and two babies be trans-ported to the island. The object was to find out which language the infants would speak as they grew up, with the hope that it would be the 'original language', or language of God. Sadly for the king, it seems the children did not speak at all.

Inchkeith has a long history of fortification in the defence of the forth and Leith, and parts of the original 16th century fort still stand. Indeed, the island is littered with the remains of ruined military structures. During the world wars the island became part of an integrated defensive structure known as Fortress Forth, and at one time nearly 1,000 men were stationed here. The island is capped by a lighthouse constructed in 1803.

Another island of interest in the Firth of Forth is Inchcolm (Island of Saint Columba). The nine hectare island sits off the south coast of Fife opposite Braefoot Bay and is separated from the mainland by a stretch of water known as Mortimer's Deep.

Inchcolm was home to a religious community linked to Saint Columba, by whom it was perhaps visited in 567AD. The Scottish king Alexander I is said to have been storm-bound on the island for three days in 1123 and, to thank the hermits who had given him

shelter, he promised to build a monastic settlement. After Alexander's death his brother David I founded an Augustinian priory, later made into an abbey in 1223. The buildings, including a square tower, a ruined church, refectory and chapter house, form the best preserved monastic house in Scotland, now in the care of Historic Scotland. To visit you'll need to take a ferry from South Queensferry.

Taking a ferry, sometimes crossing a bridge and on occasion hopping on a small aircraft will become familiar experiences as you explore the islands of Scotland. The riches of some of this planet's most alluring islands await you.

ABOVE Blackness Castle is a 15th-century fortress, near the village of Blackness, Scotland, on the south shore of the Firth of Forth

Design & Artwork: ALEX YOUNG

Published by: DEMAND MEDIA LIMITED

Publisher: JASON FENWICK

Written by: PAT MORGAN